London's Young
Entrepreneur of the Year (NatWest
GBEA) and founder of sustainable style
brand TALA and fitness tech brand Shreddy,
GRACE BEVERLEY is a successful female
entrepreneur shaking up the business world, with
a global digital reach of over 1.5 million. By the age
of just twenty-three, Grace had been named first
in *Forbes*' 30-under-30 retail and e-commerce list,
graduated from Oxford University, and attained a
Sustainable Business accreditation from Harvard
Business School. Grace's inspiring drive to
accelerate the slow-fashion space and provide
the blueprint for aspiring entrepreneurs has
led to features in *Drapers*, *Forbes*,
CEO Today, *VOGUE Business*
and *Business Insider*.

EX LIBRIS

working hard hardly working

how to achieve more, stress less and feel fulfilled

grace beverley

HUTCHINSON
LONDON

1 3 5 7 9 10 8 6 4 2

Hutchinson
20 Vauxhall Bridge Road
London SW1V 2SA

Hutchinson is part of the Penguin Random House group of companies
whose addresses can be found at global.penguinrandomhouse.com

First published in the United Kingdom by Hutchinson in 2021

www.penguin.co.uk

A CIP catalogue record for this book is available from the British Library.

ISBN 9781786332851 (Hardback)
ISBN 9781786332868 (Trade paperback)

Typeset in 11/17 pt Garamond MT Std
by Integra Software Services Pvt. Ltd, Pondicherry

Printed and bound in Great Britain by Clays Ltd, Elcograf S.p.A.

The authorised representative in the EEA is Penguin Random House Ireland, Morrison
Chambers, 32 Nassau Street, Dublin D02 YH68.

Penguin Random House is committed to a sustainable future for
our business, our readers and our planet. This book is made from
Forest Stewardship Council® certified paper.

To the future you

CONTENTS

INTRODUCTION

Like most people, I have worked here and there since being a teenager. And again like most people, I'm sure, work has come with the occasional surprise and unexpected challenge. I spent my school years competing for local babysitting rights and convincing determined middle-class parents that paying someone to supervise their child's music practice was the best way to get the most out of their already expensive lessons. The babysitting was as cushty as could be – if I was lucky, I'd arrive and the children would need minimal supervision watching cartoons or making a geography poster, then they'd get straight into bed and I'd revel in the luxury of their parents' Sky box.

The worst babysitting experience I had involved a new 'client'. Upon arrival, the family's dog somehow slipped out the front door without any of us noticing. I was being introduced to the two boys (aged two and four) when the parents yelped in horror at the realisation of their dog's immaculate Houdini impression, and darted out the door, leaving me with their seemingly harmless children. The younger boy requested a story about a dinosaur, so I settled into the playroom to read about Darren the Diplodocus, hoping the parents would find the dog – both for its own good and for my selfish desire that they'd go out and I could 'babysit' as planned.

Out of the corner of my eye, I noticed child number one waddling round the corner into the kitchen, so I paused Steven the Stegosaurus and went to retrieve him. By the time I got to him, and I'm not exaggerating *at all*, this daredevil child had prised open a child-locked door and was holding an enormous kitchen knife. In that moment, I was certain this angel-faced demon would either stab me or fall over and impale himself, framing me for his murder.

After a lucky escape for both of us, I sat the children down and mustered up my most authoritative voice, explaining just how dangerous knife-gate could have been, and that it was neither funny nor clever. (Bar, of course, the fact that I'm using it as the opening anecdote of my book.) In response to this monologue, terrible toddler two opened his tiny mouth. I awaited my apology. Instead, the words 'I need poo' came out. Jumping into action, I swiftly demanded directions to the nearest toilet, while scooping up team double-trouble under my arms. After following the infant sat-nav, I found myself at our destination: the master bedroom toilet, which, via some strange, masochistic interior design decision, was carpeted. We're talking wall to wall. I immediately saw where these children inherited their propensity for danger from.

At that moment, 'I need poo' made an unfortunate transition to 'I done poo', to which I responded, ever hopeful, 'You *need* poo?' As the child enthusiastically expressed verbal confirmation of their already existing defecation, I placed the other on the floor and began to remove poo boy's trousers. I hoped and prayed that the youth had just not yet perfected his tenses, but alas. A pungent smell wafted out of his tiny trousers, followed by a huge poo. Which fell onto the carpeted floor. As I racked my brains for recent wrongdoings that could have warranted such a drastic influx of bad karma, the older boy let out a cackle that could only be associated with impending doom, and reached, both hands outstretched, for the stool.

You'll be surprised to hear that this was, in fact, only part one of *A Babysitting Night from Hell* (sequel to this book?); I'm sparing you the rest of the details, which involved rollerblades, stairs, wall poo, a lot of Dettol, and the parents returning with canine Houdini and paying just £6 for my troubles as they'd missed their reservation and no longer needed my supervision. Instead, as this is not a book about a baby's capacity to act as the most powerful form of birth control, nor one titled *Why You Should Never Let Me Babysit Your Children*, I'll move swiftly on to how symbolic this is of our current relationship to our working lives.

While 'poo-gate' serves as great comic relief, it was also an important milestone for me: the first inkling that the reality of working life was going to be different to what I'd imagined in my hazy dreams of adulthood. And, while a particularly extreme representation, this is not unique to me; it seems to be the entire storyline of just about everyone's new working life. 'Expectation ≠ Reality', as the Instagram world would put it (directly under a collage of someone posed and perfect on the left, and the same person looking perfectly socially acceptable, but this time contorted into a shape that could only resemble a banana to demonstrate the reality of their 'stomach rolls' on the right). In most cases, our working lives take a very different form to our glossy expectations, and I'm certainly not the only person who had corporate dreams of resembling a *Suits* cast member.

The idealisation of the working world is something that I've come face to face with time and time again. When I was seventeen, I remember seeing an ad in my school bulletin for a 'social media coordinator' for a student's mother's business, and I jumped at the chance for that bit of income over the summer. I happily invoiced for every hour I spent trialling different techniques that had been developed from my experience posting strategically posed photos with strategically chosen acquaintances to my few hundred 'followers' (friends of friends). This experience set the standard for what I imagined working in social media might look like. My next foray into this brave new world starred my current Instagram account, which I started in the final year of sixth form, just after I'd turned eighteen. It was only intended to keep myself accountable while trying to get into fitness, so the account was kept private – the two friends who knew about it weren't allowed to like or follow in case of algorithm-fuelled discovery by others, and I fell out with a number of other friends who started taking the piss out of my embarrassing posts (they hit me where it hurt). It turned out that posting photos of yourself in sports bras on the internet hadn't yet caught on. At this point, this wasn't a job in any sense. I didn't post my face until I had 10,000 followers, and I didn't manage to monetise any aspect of the account until over a year and a half later.

So, a month before I started my anonymous account, I made my first few applications for 'real' jobs, opting for a fairly traditional, corporate career path. I sat verbal reasoning and critical thinking tests, attended assessment centres and interviews, and enjoyed an equal number of rejections, spots already filled, and acceptances (a roaring one of each). My sole acceptance was as a New Client Acquisition Analyst at IBM as part of their Futures 'gap year' scheme, and my thirteen-month placement would take place in a year between A-Levels and university. It would allow me to retake an A-Level, gain some experience and some much-needed savings for university, and would set me up to study something completely unrelated and, in theory, still have a head start into the corporate world. Dreamy.

Through this, and alongside my babysitting and social media adventures, my vision of what the corporate working world was like was further defined by three major reality checks: my attempt to walk around the office in heels, which lasted less than an hour; the understanding that most of my job could be done by a machine and didn't involve the slightest sliver of 'passion'; and the distinct, but mostly unacknowledged, expectation that I should be reachable at all times.

So I guess I should have known better when, about eight months before I began writing this book, I moved to London, having just graduated from university, ready to join the capital's workforce in a shiny fantasy of tailored suits. I had dreams and preconceptions about how working life would be; I imagined myself working hard and having a constant, success-fuelled spring to my step. We grow up with the idea that working and being an adult are one and the same, so when we enter the workforce, there's this expectation that suddenly everything will fall into place. The hard part is getting the job: everything after that is just the 'happily ever after'.

I realised very quickly that working every hour of every day, including weekends, and still not managing to do it 'right' was unsustainable – and also the norm. I was confronted by the reality that acting like you know more than you do is unhelpful rather than clever; that you're always going to feel like you're doing and achieving less than everyone else; and that self-care is more often finally doing things you've been putting off, like laundry or replying to that old school friend, rather than sitting back with a facemask. The rose-tinted glasses came off in a flash, revealing a different reality: everyone seemed lost, expecting passion to be their driving force, but asking themselves how the hell passion can realistically add up to forty hours a week of ticking boxes.

I don't think the disparity between our expectation of work and its reality comes simply from our fantasies of office life. To me, the problem of this 'new working world' runs much deeper.

It may come as little surprise that in my opinion social media plays a huge part in explaining why we are where we are. We cannot talk about what it's like to be in the working world of today without talking about social media. And we will, a lot. We've grown up within the attention economy, with the wealthiest and most powerful companies in the world vying – largely successfully – for our attention in every area of our lives. We're no longer simply misled by movies and TV shows, so much as we're influenced by a pre-packaged reality, sold to us through our phone screens and gift-wrapped in relatability to disguise how far-fetched it really is. There is a social-media-shaped fingerprint on the surface of how we see most things – everything from hustle to self-care to success and self-worth – and we are part of a generation that exists predominantly within an environment of hyper-comparison. This being said, it seems clear that while social media may have exacerbated a lot of these problems, it didn't invent them. As millennials and Gen Zers, we are not the first generations to compare ourselves to others, to feel the need to be the last to leave the office or to want to be seen as successful. We are, however, the first generations to be constantly and ubiquitously surrounded by these issues, and for that interconnectivity to infinitely multiply how many people we are comparing ourselves with. In this sense, social media is a magnifying glass for a lot of the issues we're facing; it both enlarges the problems, and demands their inspection.

Yet, while we shouldn't underestimate its impact, the reality is that social media is not the only culprit either. Now is a difficult time to enter the working world and all that accompanies it, and it's even harder to adapt quickly enough to a constantly changing work landscape. The social or cultural contract which defines what 'success' looks like in today's society – the one that told us that if we found a good job and worked hard, we would be able to buy a house, pay off the mortgage, and retire with some savings – is breaking down. Instead, post-2008 crash, mid-global pandemic and pre(?!)-environmental crisis, our future seems more uncertain than ever. We're staring at mass unemployment in the face, many of us are working from home for the first time, and there's a confusing paradox of both loving this newfound homely freedom and missing the workplace camaraderie (often both at the same time). As I write this, the number of people out of work in the past three months rose by 243,000 in the UK – the largest increase since May 2008. And that's not counting the 2.5 million people on the government's furlough scheme, who are currently facing unprecedented and ever-growing levels of uncertainty.

Our working world has morphed beyond recognition, dragging our expectations kicking and screaming after it. And on top of that, as the 'youth of today', we've had numerous different identities heaped upon us: snowflakes, burned out, lazy, workaholics, entitled, self-carers, hustlers. We are caught in an uncomfortable middle ground between our own expectations and reality, sandwiched between other people's opinions of us.

Being labelled entitled, workshy, and the adjective one could only imagine to be 'snowflake-y', is nothing new (she types, through hard-done-by, you-don't-understand-us tears). In a 2016 op-ed in *The Australian*, 'young people' were generation-splained (mansplaining's wider-reaching sibling), with the assertion that if we all stopped eating avocado toast with 'crumbled feta', and a seemingly insulting 'five-grain toasted bread', we could buy houses instead. Now, to provide context, I am extremely privileged to own a house – and it certainly wasn't thanks to refraining from an over-enthusiastic combination of seeds in my bread, nor from gagging myself in local independent cafés. It was because I've been a significant exception to an unfair rule – in ways we'll go into later – and my own reality is not reflective of my wider generation at all. The implication that we can't buy houses because we brunch too often is facetious at best, and damaging at worst. For one, housing is far more expensive than it was for our parents' generation. In fact, the BBC calculated that you would have to save on 24,499 servings of avocado toast to afford just an average deposit – that's over sixty-seven years of eating the avo-toast combo every single day. As much as I guiltily *love* the dish, you can very much count me out there (plus, the chances of finding a ripe avocado every day for seventy years seem pretty laughable, if you ask me). The idea that we don't have financial security because we're slacking or irresponsible is not just rude, it's also flat-out wrong. It's a classic 'in my day … ', made particularly painful by the fact that many of those spouting this nonsense are often the very people who, through their political choices, have contributed to the widening gap between wages and living costs.

And then we have the other side of the label-imposing coin: the burnout generation. In her viral article (now turned book), 'How Millennials Became the Burnout Generation', Anne Helen Petersen describes a phenomenon which seems to resonate with just about everyone: suffering a kind of paralysis when faced with even the most mundane tasks, due to having 'internalised the idea that [we] should be working all the time'. I guess the snowflake-yellers would scream 'of course they liked it', because what better way to appeal to a generation of laziness and entitlement than to tell them they're the opposite of lazy? (It's rare that lazy people like to be called lazy.) Perhaps anticipating such a response, Petersen asserted that the aim of the piece was not to exonerate, but to analyse, recognise and create a generational awareness around just why our attitudes to work are the way they are. The article is a well-researched and honest exploration of just how the fuck we got here, and I wholeheartedly support its status as a very accurate state of affairs. It argues that it's not that

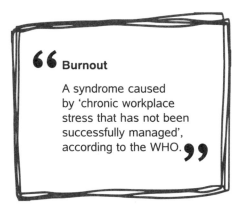

Burnout

A syndrome caused by 'chronic workplace stress that has not been successfully managed', according to the WHO.

we don't want to earn our stripes, it's also that we can't — because it's not enough to earn badges, be able to afford current housing prices or pay off student debt. It delves into how we have internalised the idea of working all the time, how we're never off the clock due to the ubiquity of our work, even if we make the bold and controversial decision to take time off.

Just twenty-one days after Petersen's article was published, Erin Griffith wrote a tangentially related article for the *New York Times* asking why young people are 'pretending to love work'. As a millennial herself, Griffith delves into a new brand of 'performative workaholism' demonstrated by her peers. She argues that our obsession with productivity has become intertwined with the search for meaning in our lives, observing that 'in San Francisco … I've noticed that the concept of productivity has taken on an almost spiritual dimension'. Perhaps we aren't working too little, then; could we be working too much?

Griffith concludes that it makes sense to pretend to love something that we're always doing. So is it a cathartic defence mechanism? My small exhale of gratification when exclaiming how *crazy* it is at work might *just about* explain the expression 'toil glamour', before I then internalise, as Petersen

> **Hustle-porn**
>
> A term I heard first at a panel I was lucky enough to film with Niran Vinod and Damola Timeyin about their book, *How to Build It*. The term says it all.

says, how we need to be working 24/7 to earn our rightful place in this hustle-porn-fuelled generation.

So while I was coming to the realisation that I had Not a Fucking Clue™ whether I was lazy, burned out, entitled, lost, working hard, hardly working or all of the above, I began to conclude that no one else did either. In a strange combination of our self-perception being warped by social-media expectations and funhouse-mirror reflections of how we're told we are, we've entered into what is not just my identity crisis, but that of an entire generation. A generation #sponsored by comparison, projection, performativity, hustle, stereotypes, confusion, close inspection of the self by the self – and by everyone else.

Following these contradictory explanations of a generation, we are led to the realisation that we may embody both sides: simultaneously burned out and also lazy snowflakes. Petersen largely concludes that we are all burned out, we are not lazy. While it might not settle the debate once and for all, perhaps it could be rephrased as 'we might be lazy, but it's because we're burned out', or 'we might be entitled, but that's because we are entitled to expectations that don't involve financial crashes, job shortages, climates ascending at an alarming rate and affordable housing as an exception to the rule'. Perhaps it also says something that I'm not even part of the millennial cohort discussed – born in 1997, I teeter on the cusp and fall into Generation Z by definition – and I'm a homeowner, yet I still feel the afflictions of our hustle culture and situationally-induced burnout. The fact that I agree with Petersen, and yet am not a millennial, does not negate her argument in the slightest. In fact, it shows just how epochal these issues stand to be – perhaps it's not just a single burnout generation we're looking at, but an entire new burnout culture created by our new working world.

Work culture used to be about 'earning stripes', but we don't want that any more. Generally, we no longer think it's necessary to sit through fifteen years of corporate work in order to know the field and move up the rankings, paying respect to the culture in return for a pension we're not even guaranteed to receive. We'd rather better our chances by trying our own luck, spurred on by side-hustle culture. We refuse to be put in a box, but suffer from the lack of boundaries that comes from moving beyond those walls of traditional benchmarks. As a generation, we've grown up without definitive borders between work and 'not-work'. Technology allows us constant access to our working lives, which has slowly but surely developed into an anxiety that *not* working anywhere and everywhere is the equivalent of being in the office and having a nap. We have a sort of paradox of choice – the ability to monetise each and every hobby we might employ, and yet the insistence that if we aren't earning stripes, we're cutting corners.

In his 2019 article, 'The Toxic Fantasy of the Side Hustle', Alex Collinson asks when we started saying 'side-hustle', rather than just 'second job'. The article was part of a slew of online examinations following Henley Business School's 2018 study on the side-hustle economy, and I think that the notion of it being a 'toxic fantasy' is pretty bang on. It's not that the impression of having a side-hustle is necessarily misleading, and it's certainly not *wrong* by any means, but the fantasy of it is misplaced. The side-hustle feeds off the idea that we all have an unlimited potential for earning money, restricted only by our time and what we choose to do with it. As Jenny Odell puts it so

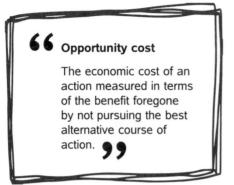

" Opportunity cost

The economic cost of an action measured in terms of the benefit foregone by not pursuing the best alternative course of action. **"**

well in her book *How to do Nothing,* 'Every moment of every day is a financial resource to be captured, optimised, and appropriated.' With this thinking, the opportunity cost of spending time doing anything *other than work* is suddenly really fucking high.

Relaxing? You could be earning.

Walking the dog? Could be getting paid for it.

Donating clothes to charity? Should've flogged them on eBay.

On your phone? You could be making thousands in stocks and shares as a #forex #trader.

I'll be the first to put my hand up and say that I have started my career through side-hustles, and they've brought me great rewards. There's nothing wrong with having a side-hustle – it would be hypocritical of me to say otherwise – but there are significant questions to be asked about the impact of it as a culture. It's become an illustrious dream that turns any second you're not earning money into an anxiety, and the mental effects of that are draining.

As I write this in the midst of a global pandemic, we're feeling the fear more than ever. Our isolation within our home-office hybrids has led to viral shame, directly linking our self-worth to our ability, not only to adapt, but also to become some sort of productivity machine so that somehow, when all this passes, we are not only alive and virus-free, but also ten years ahead of our peers, trilingual, oh, and a national hero. In what *Contagion*-style movie did we think the main plot line would be Susan finally starting her own business instead of, you know, simply surviving while locked in her house attempting to escape a potentially deadly virus? It has become impossible to go online without being bombarded with ideals about what you should be doing hour-upon-hour, and the assertion that this unprecedented time is your opportunity to recalibrate and put your wildest dreams into action. This is not a curse, they tell us, this is a chance, and if you don't take it you're *choosing* not to succeed.

I'd now like to introduce Team Productivity to Team Self-Care – the co-dependent realities of this world. On the other side of the hustle-gram feed, you're given resolution. You're told to sit back, relax, slow down, press pause. You're told that the outside world will still be waiting for you and that you should take this opportunity to rest. You're told that you should embrace boredom because it's a privilege. So you do, press pause, that is, even though the only vaguely impressive thing you've accomplished today is finishing that new Netflix series, which you didn't even enjoy that much because your to-do list is far more dramatic than the protagonist.

Let me explain where I'm coming from.

In August 2019, before the pandemic initiated a mass office exodus, I started working from home, and what I had thought would be an ideal lifestyle was anything but. I found myself feeling stuck in the house, yet unable to leave. I was at my least productive but spending the most time working. There seemed to be no midpoint between these two extremes, as though I was a scale tipping from one side to the other, constantly verging on capsize. I just didn't understand – working from home is a luxury! You get to have your meetings in pyjamas, your colleague is your very cute dog, and there's an unlimited supply of snacks. But despite all the perks, I found myself falling into a spiral of uncreativity and poor mental health, feeling my life revolved around to-do lists with no purpose. I soon realised that I was balancing it all wrong, creating a routine where there was no middle ground between working so hard that I didn't leave the house for days and lunch breaks were an ancient memory, and doing so little that what should have been an hour of admin would drift aimlessly into an early lunch, and then never really being able to get back into the swing of things. I was doing everything but getting nowhere.

All of this brewed together in a cauldron of self-doubt and I began to think that maybe I was just lazy, that I didn't know the first thing about work. I was working hard, putting in the hours, yet I felt I was achieving nothing and I was *miserable*. How could my self-perceived hard work and diligence have transformed into a mastery of unproductivity?

I started to realise that either I was incurably burned out at the ripe old age of twenty-two, or that I had to step back from my pre-conceived notions of what 'hard work' is and instead figure out how *I* work. I listened to what made me feel good, helped me work hard, and got me rewards, and within a few months I'd learned how to understand myself. I discovered what kept me motivated, what inspired me, what pushed me to continue when motivation couldn't be found, and formulated what was a sustainable and productive routine for myself. A crash course where the three classes were me, myself and I. I'm not a lazy person because some days I can't – and don't want to – motivate myself. I'm just a human who didn't see the comfort found in separating work and home, who didn't understand that cancelling plans in the evening because you're already home and closer to bed is completely valid and not anti-social, even if it makes you feel worse. What I learned from my work-from-home struggles was how to know myself, my boundaries and shortcomings, and it changed my life and my productivity: my work was better in quality and quantity, and so was my time off.

So when the Covid-19 pandemic hit in March 2020, and many people began working from home for the first time, I posted an Instagram story in which I shared a 'work-from-home' tip. I recommended that people who struggle to concentrate after lunch watch a TED Talk during their break and give it their full attention. For me, this distracts enough from my work to give me a much-needed break, without the risk of falling into a full-on YouTube hole which ends up with me being so engrossed in an instruction video on how to make an Ikea elfstödt into a loo roll holder that I miss my 3pm call. The tip was well received by those in need of help due to the change in environment, but it went down like a lead balloon with the *this-is-a-pandemic-not-a-productivity-contest* camp. Of course, I stand wholeheartedly by the sentiments of both parties. I wanted to shout from the rooftops how much I agreed, and how out of touch these 'if you don't come out of lockdown with ____, you never lacked time, you just lacked discipline' posts are. But equally, I have to be productive for my own mental health sometimes. Above anything else, that's what was helping me through and keeping me sane at that moment.

My tip was a personal one, aimed at helping those who might need it and intended to be ignored by those who felt differently. Instead, the camps went to war: productivity versus self-care, round fifty, *ding ding*. But where is the equilibrium to be found in this battle? Is there a middle ground we can use to know when to push forwards and when to step back? The question should not be: do you care about your work and being successful, or do you care about your mental health and social life? You need to be able to care about both – work fulfilment and self-fulfilment. And I'm not talking about 'having it all', that reverberating echo from eighties feminism gone by. It's about knowing what you want and when you want it, and learning how to harness the merits of both productivity and self-care to treat yourself less like a machine, and more like the complex human you are. Surely, in this battle of the camps, there is a way in which we can take a look deep down at who we are, what we need, where we want to be, and come out on top. It is clear that neither side can win outright from an objective standpoint – how can it be blanket-applied to the entire population? We're not all the same. The important thing is understanding what works for you personally, and being able to consume advice accordingly.

Aside from learning never to post on social media without disclaimers, what sharing that story taught me was that I wasn't the only one having a crisis. Just as I appeared very much aboard the hustle train to the outside world while actually struggling in private, others were facing similar hurdles without anyone else realising. And, once the realisation hit me, I began to see it everywhere. Scrolling through my newsfeed, I noticed I was being told to stand up and sit down at the same time – to *relax*, because it's important to look after myself, then, two thumb-metres down, to *hustle* and only sleep when I'm dead! Yay! I came to the conclusion that we are wedged not between a rock and a hard place, but a *127 Hours*-style cliff, towering over us on both sides. Thankfully, rather than cutting off our limbs, what we desperately need is to work out what this generational contradiction actually means, and how to reframe self-care and productivity for our own benefit.

We are stuck in this constant battle when instead we could harness our potential (in whatever direction that may be) by understanding our own strengths, boundaries, desires and downfalls. It seems that the only way in which we can fully comprehend the complexity of this discussion is by looking into ourselves and finding out what productivity means to us, what our 'purpose' is, if such a thing exists, and what makes us feel most whole, even if that's getting to the weekend and paying our bills. It comes down to truly knowing ourselves, so that we know when it is time to get on and do something, and when to put the laptop down and walk away. We are the only ones who can work this out for ourselves, which is why the 'winner takes all' outlook completely misses the point.

In truth, productivity and success feed off the idea of balance. Yet the idea of balance finds itself – often sarcastically, with an aggressively raised eyebrow – sitting within the 'be kind to yourself' club, teetering into a justification for putting on a facemask instead of finishing that project you started. Being productive means knowing when to push yourself that little bit harder, when to carry on working, as well as when to rest and recuperate. What I hope you'll get from this book is a 'productivity blueprint' to help you navigate our strange working world, in which productivity and self-care become one and the same, rather than forcing people to identify with one or the other. Because sometimes productivity can be a form of self-care, and sometimes self-care is the most productive thing we can do.

So that's why we're here, having a conversation about work and productivity, and how to make both more meaningful. And I guess you're here for exactly that, no matter whether or not you knew me before picking up this book. This book has been a passion project and a half – a painful exploration mixed with truths I probably would never have had the energy to talk about online. It's required me to deep-dive into my fears and desires and create what I hope will resonate with my weird and wonderful generation. This is my account – my tips, my exploration, my truths. This is how *I* see purpose, productivity, passion, self-worth, success, social media, enjoyment, fulfilment, life.

But it's not a memoir, and I hope it holds as much value as if it weren't written by 'influencer and entrepreneur' Grace. I want you to read it as if it's not me talking, because it's not really about me; this is about you now having a conversation with yourself about what *you* really want – your fears, your dreams, your happiness. That is how you'll get the most out of this book, even if it means you vehemently disagree with some (or all) of the things I say.

No one has all the answers. No one, *not one person*, is perfect – by your standards, by theirs, or by anyone else's. A short temper, a bad attitude, vulnerability – *something* has to give. We're human, we're flawed, and our expectations are the most flawed of all. So please don't think I've got it all figured out. The sooner we can withdraw from that comparison-based thinking, the closer we are to giving ourselves the chances we give to others, while also striving for self-improvement where we desire it. Create a fair playing field, in your own mind above all, so that these conversations are productive, and so that you can analyse your own behaviours and feelings without assuming that you're the only one that falls down in the areas that you do.

I've also made the slightly radical decision (that should not be radical at all), not to write solely for womxn in this book. At the beginning it started as that, because all business books written by women seem to be aimed specifically at women, but (and this is a big juicy but), women should not have to write solely for women when writing about work or business, or anything at all. We should not just be marketed to ourselves. When I'm talking about the work landscape, I'm talking about the work landscape. I hope we're at the point now where a man doesn't feel emasculated when taking advice or reading thoughts by a woman. I think if we're not at that point, then those leaving themselves out are missing out on a really important conversation. My aim is to write, as a woman, for the new generation, and for those wanting to understand the new generation.

INTRODUCTION

The first part of the book – *Working Hard* – is focused around the world of work. Think of it as a journey, one that looks at our working lives as more than just a single-track towards our own and society's standards of success. We'll discuss deciding on your journey (purpose and passion), how to make the journey work for you (productivity and time management), enjoying the journey (flow and creativity), and creating destinations along the way (defining success). I've tried to present a holistic view of the world of work now and what that means for each of us, without the usual preconceptions of what we should be doing when, how and why – and how this amounts to somehow 'doing life properly'.

The second part of the book – *Hardly Working* – is every bit as important as the first, which might seem strange in a 'productivity blueprint' for the new working world. But that's the point – productivity and self-care are two sides of the same coin. One does not exist without the other. In this section, we'll redefine productivity to include that radical act of non-work, and reframe it as a tool to incite fulfilment and personal success in our work and lives. If you want more assurance as to why this is so important – or if you're considering just reading the first part – flip to Chapter 5 right after you finish this introduction. That's the linchpin that holds this whole concept together. In the rest of the section we'll talk about 'having it all' – balancing everything from work to play to refuting expectations and creating realistic but genuine success – and the crucial art of doing nothing. I hope this book will help you to play to your strengths and cope with your weaknesses – all in a world that celebrates the former and commoditises the latter.

If I had my way, I'd recommend you read the book in order, flagging any areas that made you think or feel a certain way so you can return to them. I know you're not meant to write in books (apologies to my school librarian), but you'll know a book is my favourite if it's annotated to the heavens. It's about the feeling a certain passage or chapter has incited in me and being able to create that feeling again whenever I want it: whenever I want to be inspired, or reassured, or motivated, or at peace. I never feel the same two days in a row, but the reality of work is that sometimes you need to get the fuck on and do something, and sometimes you need to convince yourself that relaxation is the most productive thing you can do. You have my blessing to use this book as a notebook – to turn down corners and write in pen and make it your own. That's the whole point.

So, I guess we should get into it.

working hard

CHAPTER ONE

FINDING YOUR PURPOSE

We're told that we're a generation fuelled by purpose. And, to be fair to us, that is a great thing. 'Purpose-driven leadership' shines bright on my LinkedIn profile, to celebrate a recently completed online business school course. My businesses centre around their 'why' to an extent that I am continuously proud of. We're a conscientious generation. More than ever, we care about substance over style and meaning over method. Or at least we try to, wherever we can.

But I believe we've lost our way when it comes to how we treat purpose. Or maybe it's the way it's sold as a concept that rubs me up the wrong way. Stripping everything else away, the word 'purpose' has two semi-distinct definitions. A quick Google search tells me that purpose either means 'the reason for which something is done' (enter the term, 'purpose-driven'), or 'a person's sense of resolve or determination'. To me, that says that 'purpose' can be easily split into two concepts, one that is goal-orientated and one that is process-orientated. Nothing wrong there.

So why is it that whenever I hear someone telling us to find a job we love in order to never work a day in our lives, my eyes automatically defy gravity and roll swiftly back into my head? When I think, for a second, about this superior ideal of 'purpose', for some reason I don't think of a doctor, or a humanitarian worker, but the sparkly, aspirational, purpose-driven lifestyle of a young Instagrammer. They might be a life coach or a foreign exchange trader. They're definitely on a beach or by a pool (minimum twenty storeys above sea-level). There's either no laptop in sight or there's a sleek piece of tech dangerously close to the aforementioned body of water, for perilous contrast. Now, there's nothing wrong with their jobs – I'm sure they're doing them very well and paving the way for hosts of others to build a similar sort of life. But it's the caption, which tells me and my fellow viewers that they're so glad they left their dead-end, 'average' job for a life of constant luxury and infinite, unwavering contentment, that triggers in me an emotion that I can only represent with a sarcastic thumbs up.

The myth that paints purpose front and centre of any working-life-worth-living is just that: *triggering*. I don't think that we're necessarily sold purpose more than the generations before us, but we *are* sold aspirations on an unprecedented level. 'Living the dream' is our currency when it comes to sellability online, and it is this *flaunting* of fulfilled purpose that is the problem. If the internet had been around thirty years ago, it might very well have been chock full of aesthetically pleasing quotations declaring that 'the purpose of life is a life of purpose' – it is, after all, a lovely sentiment. But the difference now is the unbreakable connection we've drawn between purpose and work, which has inverted the work → money → purpose trajectory and placed purpose right at the beginning of our earliest career steps, declaring it a necessity rather than a luxury.

Following the general labelling of millennials as the 'purpose-driven generation', peer coaching platform Imperative ran a LinkedIn survey in which it quizzed participants on the importance of money, purpose and status as employment attributes. Perhaps surprisingly, the data showed that the older the participant, the more purpose-driven they seemed to be: 48 per cent of baby boomers in the survey were purpose-oriented, compared to 30 per cent of millennials and 38 per cent of Gen Z participants. To me, this is simply the logical path of fulfilling *needs* first and progressing to *wants* once you are established in your working life. Is it any wonder, then, that we find it overwhelming being lumped with the importance of all three – money, purpose and status – from the off? Our treatment of the concept of purpose has evolved from a preference to do meaningful and passion-filled work, to one that must both be hyper-fulfilling and hyper-lucrative.

The marketing of this purpose ideal as an aspirational must-have has replaced a natural desire to find meaning and enjoyment in our working lives with the anxiety that, if you're living anything less than this financially, morally and emotionally superior way of life, you're doing it all wrong. It's a modern vocational representation of Dr Russ Harris's *The Happiness Trap*. Dr Harris argues that happiness is presented to us as a 'reachable', constant, stable, always-peaked state, without acknowledging that a crucial part of happiness is experiencing it through a range of emotions. In a similar sense, we seem to have fallen deep into a purpose trap, laid out for us by those who make us feel we should be constantly happy and constantly fulfilled in our jobs, which we love at all times because we have drunk from the holy grail of purpose. And this isn't just found in happy-go-scammy lifestyles, but in the entire conversation that paints 'purpose' as a static end goal in our work.

Combine this with our hustle-happy culture, and the logical conclusion is that, if purpose is the goal, and purpose is found through your vocation, then work is the never-ending reality.

The reality of purpose is much more complex than pursuing some end goal we pick as teenagers, jump into as soon as we begin working, and hold on to throughout our lives. After all, how are we meant to know our life-long purpose at fourteen, when we whittle down our GCSEs towards specialisms? (I was determined that I'd be a lawyer or politician, not sure how well the posting of bikini photos and slightly inappropriate memes would've gone down there.) How are we expected to have some big sense of our purpose when we finish education and enter the workforce, when we're still just learning the rules of the game? Quite simply, we aren't: we just can't.

What I want to encourage is a shift in perspective, from thinking of our lives as having *one* goal – which should also make us the money we need to survive and bring us the success we crave – to filling them with a variety of passions that change and develop as we do. Even if you truly believe you have an overarching purpose that is tied to the work you do, surely there are endless other elements of your life that you enjoy and want to cultivate. It is by indulging in this multiplicity that we can more easily decipher when to lean in and work harder, when to sit back and relax, and when to re-evaluate our direction. We learn to celebrate the small wins, and ultimately get greater fulfilment from our everyday lives. With the modern world putting so many non-negotiable purposes in place for us (living to work), surely we can fill in the remaining gaps with a variety of passions rather than feeling inferior for not having it all sussed.

Assigning a single purpose to your life and expecting that to solve all your problems is like having only one friend who you call on for everything:

going out, staying in, crying, laughing, work troubles, family issues … the list goes on. While some might be lucky enough to have a friend like that, the majority of us will have multiple people in our lives at any one time, who we rely on at different moments, who grow and develop alongside us. We might lose some along the way and gain others: that's life. Similarly, there are many different areas of our life, both in and out of work, that need to be nurtured in order for us to feel fulfilled. Because, at the end of the day, fulfilment and ongoing contentment is what we're all aiming for, whatever that might mean to you.

You might be wondering why we're jumping straight in to *Life's Big Questions* – and, quite frankly, it's because the conversation has gone that way. Capitalism, exacerbated by hustle-porn, has sold us the idea of a single purpose as a way of chaining our identity to our work so that we grind harder, placing the emphasis on achieving our #goals rather than adopting healthy working practices. In the long term, this is unrealistic and damaging, especially when we're expected to work through a maze of newly invented careers with the goalpost of retirement constantly moving. However you might feel about capitalism, it's important to understand it as the landscape we are operating within, because it affects everything we do: how we feel about success, what makes us feel fulfilled, whether we believe that to be legitimate or whether it's 'just a hobby'.

By bringing purpose into the modern day, we can shape it to suit *us* rather than letting it dictate our lives. I like to think of my purpose as layered, nuanced and ever-changing. One day, that might mean creating something amazing or doing something humanitarian; on another day it might mean getting through meetings without falling asleep. And this spans beyond each individual day – we all have stages of life where we have to push through shit we hate in order to take steps forwards. It frees us to create a life we love,

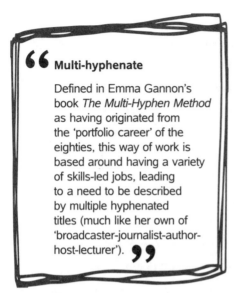

❝ Multi-hyphenate

Defined in Emma Gannon's book *The Multi-Hyphen Method* as having originated from the 'portfolio career' of the eighties, this way of work is based around having a variety of skills-led jobs, leading to a need to be described by multiple hyphenated titles (much like her own of 'broadcaster-journalist-author-host-lecturer'). ❞

whether that's as a multi-hyphenate or in a traditional nine to five. In this sense, my purpose is my *lack* of a singular purpose, which allows me to work with smaller, temporary goals and to identify when I need to pursue things I'm not passionate about in order to enhance my work.

What I'm trying to say is that we need to move the discussion away from goal-orientated purpose and towards **self-actualisation**.

I first discovered the term 'self-actualisation' used in a modern sense in Phoebe Lovatt's *The Working Woman's Handbook* (a fantastic book full of practical advice which I highly recommend), when she interviews author and former *Teen Vogue* editor Elaine Welteroth. 'We all have an obligation to self-actualise,' Welteroth states. 'That is your singular goal on this planet: if you feel like you are meant to be here for a certain reason, you *have* to follow that.'

I *really* didn't get the concept at first. In fact, I found it pretty counterproductive. I read 'singular goal' and instantly thought, 'Here is yet another person preaching the superiority of instant, early adopted "purpose".' Despite the qualifying 'if' in her statement, it still felt as though she was describing an ultimate goal, one in which passion reigns supreme and which we *need* to chase after at all times (as if that's always possible, and nothing can get in the way). So, as I do when I read about seriously in-depth psychological theories instead of *Teen Vogue* (which is definitely all the time), I decided to research the concept further.

The term 'self-actualisation' stems from Maslow's well-known 'Hierarchy of Needs'. It's very likely that the idea for his now-famous triangle was developed from his observation of the indigenous Blackfoot Nation whose traditional tipis symbolised how self-actualisation forms the basis on which community actualisation is built. In shifting much of their emphasis from the community on to the individual, Maslow placed self-actualisation at the top of his pyramid of needs, whereby we reach complete fulfilment. But, says Maslow, this point is rarely – if ever – reached, and even then would only be possible once everything else has been taken care of: food, water, physical and psychological safety, intimate human relationships, and a feeling of esteem and accomplishment. In this context I agreed with Welteroth's sentiment that self-actualising – as a constant pursuit of fulfilment, whether reachable or not – is something we should be striving for. But with purpose having climbed down from the top to the bottom of the pyramid, we're suddenly burdened with the pressure that our work has to fulfil so many needs at once, all the time. So, as I learned more about the development of self-actualisation over time, applying it to modern-day working life started to present some very intriguing solutions to the problem of purpose.

A simple dictionary definition search of self-actualisation tells us that it is: 'The realisation or fulfilment of one's talents and potentialities, especially considered as a drive or need present in everyone.'

Now, I'm not usually in the habit of borrowing theories from psychologists, but to me, if we translate this into the modern day, the act of self-actualising becomes the pursuit of passions of all shapes and sizes, in work and in life. Precisely because we've brought the ultimate goal of fulfilling purpose down to our more basic needs, we need to start thinking of it as an action that you *do* (self-actualis*ing*) rather than a thing you *have* (self-actualis*ation*) for it to be a useful tool. If you make an effort to self-actualise throughout your work, you're engaging in the concept constantly, realising and fulfilling at an everyday level, rather than aiming for one final destination of 'realisation' and 'fulfilment' and feeling less-than because you haven't got there yet. In that sense, self-actualising is an accumulation of things that fulfil our passions – which can be as small as chatting to people we love or as large as a career in fashion design.

It makes sense then that when Welteroth quotes Eve Ewing saying that 'there's no glory in a grind that literally grinds you down to dust', she doesn't mean that there is one ultimate peak which we grind towards and which, because we love it so much, never feels like work. Instead, we have a duty to ourselves to litter our work with things that we love, and follow larger passions where we have them. For me, her line highlights the importance of discovering purpose and passion *within* our everyday work and life. It's about doing our best to pursue those moments as much as we can, while understanding that this will not always bring us instant joy, and that's just part of being a working human.

The more I think about it, the more I see self-actualising as a gradual approach to work and life as a whole, far more nuanced and layered than any old-fashioned, newly warped idea of purpose. 'To work' is a verb. We treat it like it's an object, but it's something that we *do*, and in order to enjoy it, the joy has to be embedded in the process. I truly believe that this makes the notion of purpose more accessible, by redefining it completely. It does away with the idea that your lifelong aim is to do a job you love, one that will constantly bring you joy and success (and money to pay the rent), and instead provides a realistic way to discover enjoyment and passion in your work, whether or not your career *is* your passion. I'm not saying that you should settle in a job you hate, just because you can add a small element that you enjoy, or that you need to have some burning passion to pursue in order to make your work worth it. The beauty of self-actualising is that it can show us how to make our work *work for us,* and how to find happiness in the process, while acknowledging that work isn't something you're going to leap out of bed for *every single day.* It allows for a healthy relationship with the working world we know today, and gives us a sense of hope that's not misguided.

Needless to say, struggling with 'purpose' is a particularly privileged problem to face. The idea of purpose-driven work is in itself a white collar, middle-class concept. There is definitely something in our culture that reveres this glossy 'freelancer' way of working and that has lost respect for or isn't platforming good old-fashioned hard work. Due to, rather than in spite of, this, I find the discussion important. It's something that is destabilising for a large number of people, not only when they reach the top of Maslow's 'Hierarchy'. There is an extraordinary amount of choice in our work and lives now compared to fifty years ago: how we work, who we work for, industries and jobs that never existed before which seem to be popping up on a daily basis. We're now constantly bombarded with the new 'it' job (I particularly loved Emma Gannon's list of weird jobs that were up for grabs – anyone down for 'Head of Vibes'?), leaving us confused and overwhelmed, and then we're told that we should feel empowered by this choice. It's really no wonder we feel so lost in attempting to identify our purpose, and then for bonus points we throw in the shame of it being our fault if we don't make it happen because there are (literally) endless opportunities out there.

The most disorienting part of it all is that, while we have more choice than ever before, we also have an incredibly narrow view of what fulfilment at work looks like. What is wrong with wanting to work your shift, pay your bills, and still have the time and energy to go out with friends? Why do we attach some sort of moral superiority to following one big passion, rather than accepting the fact that this is often not realistic, and also not what many people *actually* want to do with their lives. Wanting to work and earn money in order to have the financial freedom to live our life to the fullest is an extraordinarily valid thing to do, and it's a much more common situation than deciding to pursue your dream of becoming an avant-garde lederhosen designer. So why do we view the desire to be financially secure as less-than? Is it because we believe this alone cannot be our purpose? In a capitalist society, how is it that we shame people who cannot – or, even more radically, *choose not to* – bring together their grand passion and the thing they do to make money? The way I see it, the only way we can do justice to the way we work is to insert smaller passions into the everyday, rather than try to fit the complexity of our everyday needs into a single passion.

There's lots we can learn from our parents' generation that we seem to have forgotten in our rush to find the perfect, purpose-filled career. We can learn to find passion within our work, even when that work exists to pay the bills. We can assess our social-media and technology-fuelled addiction to instant gratification that has led us to only do things we love, and avoid everything we hate like the plague. We can benefit tremendously from the discipline of honing our craft and shaping it to our strengths. But at the same time, we can – and often do – reject an old-fashioned view that change is bad and fickle. Now, more than ever, we are empowered to embrace change and trust that 'changing' jobs often doesn't mean giving up, but rather moving forwards. A focus on self-actualising means that time spent learning and discovering is never wasted, even if we switch paths. It's all part of the journey, as clichéd as it may sound; as we grow, it's normal that our passions and values do too.

This is all well and good, I hear you say, *but how the hell do I introduce self-actualisation into my working life?* Think of it as a long-term accumulation of different passions: if you have enough things in your day that you feel passionate about, then, in theory, you've found the key to self-actualising.

These can vary from temporary interests to passions spanning whole industries and careers, but once we find them, in Welteroth's words, it is our duty to explore and tend to them. We have to ask ourselves what we love, what makes us tick or, quite honestly, just what we can happily get lost in in today's world of external distraction.

Now, you might be reading this and worry that you have no passions (and you wouldn't be the only one). As a society, when we hear the word 'passion', we almost always think of something creative: music, art, design, film, photography, acting, dancing – you get the gist. We tend to view creative passions as the most 'valid', and can often be dismissive of any other kind. Surely someone's passion can't *really* be problem-solving? And if it is? How boring.

We need to widen the scope of what passion means. I think of it as interests or tasks that, when we engage with them, get us into a flow and give us that satisfying sense of fulfilment. For example, I *love* to conceptualise. Mind-maps are my crack. I love coming up with a concept from a single idea, putting my phone away and getting stuck into it. I would qualify mind-mapping as a micro-passion – an activity that could fit within any job – as compared to a macro-passion – an area of interest like fashion design or dance. I mind-map when I'm coming up with a marketing campaign, designing a collection, or even developing a new way of reporting to my team (I even

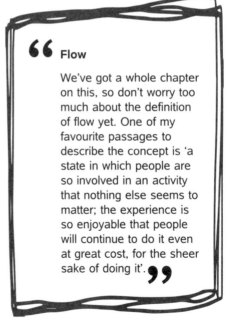

66 **Flow**

We've got a whole chapter on this, so don't worry too much about the definition of flow yet. One of my favourite passages to describe the concept is 'a state in which people are so involved in an activity that nothing else seems to matter; the experience is so enjoyable that people will continue to do it even at great cost, for the sheer sake of doing it'. 99

found a way to incorporate it into my Excel-exclusive reporting job at IBM – one of my greatest achievements to date). You probably already know what your macro-passions are, but you might be finding it harder to decipher your micros. What makes you lose track of time? It could be talking to interesting people, designing a graphic, telling a story. *These* are your micro-passions.

To me, the slightly daunting idea of 'passions' becomes digestible when I look at it as a short and long game. In the short term, doing tasks you love leads to a feeling of fulfilment – when you leave work after getting lost in something all day, you'll always feel more fulfilled. When this is applied on a long-term basis, we start to talk less about sporadic fulfilment and more about self-actualising. It seems that by including a variety of these micro- and macro-passions into your everyday, you start self-actualising over time. I don't believe there's a qualifying 10,000 hours as such, but you'll be able to feel it – perhaps you already do, or can think of a time where you got closer and closer to long-term fulfilment. As I said before, it's inevitable that all jobs include parts we hate. You don't become immune to bad moods and stress wrinkles just because you're in an industry you're passionate about, we all know that.

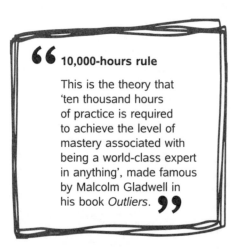

❝ 10,000-hours rule

This is the theory that 'ten thousand hours of practice is required to achieve the level of mastery associated with being a world-class expert in anything', made famous by Malcolm Gladwell in his book *Outliers*. **❞**

In reality, macro-passions are usually made up of lots of micro-passions, and that's *why* we love them. It's very rare that we love the industry or the outcome without also loving the process. We might all agree that being a doctor is a good job, and you might believe it *is* your purpose. But unless you also love the practical side of it, you're not going to enjoy being a doctor.

I loved the idea of being on the corporate ladder (and the remuneration) when I thought about my shiny fantasy of working at IBM, but when it came down to it, I didn't enjoy the process so it never added up. Had I stayed there, I would have had to take on a significant amount of extra work in order to implement my micro-passions, and it's likely it would have become unsustainable. Making sure we have micro-passions in our everyday – some days more than others – allows us to get further in the things we love, especially when working on things we hate in the short term (e.g. mandatory qualifications, chasing invoices, paying taxes).

Now, beyond the theory, this all becomes a bit self-help-that-isn't-helpful. So, how can you become better at self-actualising in a practical sense? You probably already do this a lot more than you realise. We're pretty good at doing more of what we love, even without changing our whole lives. It's in our self-gratifying nature.

STEP ONE: Look at your current situation
- What do you spend time doing that you enjoy?
- What comes to mind when you think of what you do not enjoy doing?
- Think of a time when you ended your workday happy – what happened that day?
- When you've left work drained, deflated and even upset, what do you think caused that?

STEP TWO: Consider your options
- Is there a way you could do more of the things you love in your current role? Some suggestions for how to do this might be:
  o Extra training to improve your skills.

o Take on more responsibility in that area. Note that, at least initially, this will mean an extra workload as you won't normally be able to immediately offload other work, so consider whether this is something you really want.

- If you find yourself struggling to self-actualise at work even after completing the above and analysing your smallest micro-passions, it might be time to start looking for a change.

  o Before you make a drastic decision, ask yourself: do you really need to look elsewhere?

    - Is there a role you see someone doing within your team that you think you'd love? What is it about that role that's different to yours?

    - Can you speak to your manager and try to shape your role differently to better include some of your micro-passions?

  o If the answer to both the questions above is 'no', then you should seriously consider looking elsewhere. In order to help you find a role in which you're more likely to be self-actualising, look back at your answers to Step One and ask yourself: is there a job where you can do more of that?

    In order to ensure you're making the right decision and avoid falling into the same trap again, ask yourself:

    - Why did you pick your current job in the first place?

    - What requirements do you need to consider (financial security, locations, etc.)?

    OR:

    - Is there a job that won't eat up your entire life, but allows you to turn up, make your living, and then spend the rest of your life outside of work self-actualising?

It makes more than enough sense that you'll ask yourself these questions multiple times throughout your life (cue huge sigh when that extra pile of tedious work lands on your desk at 5pm) and that seems to be the answer to making it work. We are changing beings – we cannot expect to be in a static state of happiness when we're constantly growing. Now more than ever it is wholly expected that sometimes we will move in one direction and our career will go in another; it's up to us to confront and control that as much as possible. I want to make it clear that I'm not saying you should never complain and always be happy with what you're doing, even if you loathe your job, nor that you should rush out the door and leave your work in search of the self-actualising life. It's nuanced (sick of that word yet?), and only you can decide. The beauty of self-actualising is its plurality and its subjectivity – in a world that loves nothing more than blanket statements, your self-actualising is uniquely *yours*. It allows you to view what has become a convoluted, confusing working world through your own subjective lens, and more confidently make changes to improve your life, and equally, spend less time worrying that you have to change your whole life for your work to be valid and fulfilling. It may take a little time to work out what helps you to self-actualise, and what that is will also likely change – but, crucially, it'll change *alongside* you. Let's make a commitment, right here, to stop being so intent on applying one-track, linear goals and purposes to our lives. We are complex beings, and our world isn't getting any simpler.

All this extends to our world beyond work, too. While it's incredibly important to find areas of your day job that you enjoy, self-actualisation shouldn't *only* come from your working life. Knowing what makes you fulfilled and happy in all different areas of your day is essential to feeling like you're truly living life. It seems almost too obvious to say that when you do more of what you love – no matter the context – your quality of life improves. Now, I'm not saying you should start creating PowerPoint pitches to present to your friends just because you're the pitch-master at work, or that your work phone should be sellotaped to your palm at all times because yOu lOvE yOuR jOb, but the concept of flow is just as applicable outside the office as it is inside, and we'll look at this further in Chapter 3. Reading, watching good films, laughing with friends, playing, listening to music, cooking – these are all things that might get you into your flow. Some of the most meaningful things we can do in life – humanitarian work, taking care of loved ones – are often not monetisable (even though we might wish they were). You might end up with a 50/50 working hard/hardly working self-actualising split, or it might be skewed one way or the other – the important thing is that you find yourself self-actualising to some degree both within and outside of your work. That's the first rule of balance: not to be exactly equal on both sides, but to litter all areas of your life with things you love to do, see, experience.

Self-actualising doesn't suddenly mean that we walk around with a halo-like aura, skin like a baby's bottom, cheeks glowing from constant fulfilment. If you've come here for that, all I can tell you is that you're never going to find it. You are human after all. What we *can* do is learn to understand ourselves, our working habits, our downfalls and our boundaries, and base our lives around those.

The important thing is that self-actualising opens up our whole view of success. Much like purpose, 'success' is largely defined by what society tells us it is from the day we're born. Whichever road you choose to embark on, or even if you create your own road, at some point someone, or something, will tell you what the finish line looks like, will try to define for you the end-goal you have to reach to know that *you've made it*. When you're a lawyer, you become Partner; when you're a woman, you settle down with a partner and have healthy and successful (yawn) children; when you're in the business sector, you become CEO of a multi-national corporation. In a life that never stops moving, where the clock never stops ticking, it's bizarre that we view success as static and objective. When we move the concept of purpose to that of valuing fulfilment in the everyday rather than rushing to reach a vague notion of ultimate success, we are robbing society of that power and taking it into our own hands. That's our shift to make.

So long as you focus on what helps *you* to self-actualise, and you're honest with yourself about what that is, the power to establish your own version of success is automatically in your hands. We cannot look at the world, see how much it's changed in the past fifty years, and still truly think the only ways success can be achieved are through set boundaries – becoming a parent, being a bestselling author, having a seven-figure investment account. Sure, those things can exist *alongside* self-actualising, and they can be *your* goals – but they are never the *only* goals. Self-actualising redefines traditional success and purpose within a new working world, and *that* is the whole point. That is the difference. That then frames the rest of what we do, whether that's working hard or hardly working, because where self-actualising is the goal, both are part of the journey.

What this all means is that we need to be productive to some degree in order to self-actualise. That doesn't always mean grinding hard, and we'll come back to how loaded 'productivity' is as a term, but it does mean we need to be moving, even if that's in the direction of a better mental state by shutting the laptop and sitting back. I'm not saying we should only do things we love 'because self-actualisation tOlD mE sO', but rather that we should be consciously taking steps to self-actualise more, whether that involves sitting through sleep-inducing uni lectures to qualify for a job we can more easily self-actualise in, or getting our head down and writing an application.

When I said earlier that sometimes being productive is the best form of self-care, this is partly what I was referring to.

What I want to help you achieve with this section is not productivity for productivity's sake, but a blueprint to help you work harder in order to be productive in the right direction: one of purpose, passion and self-actualising.

CHAPTER TWO

THE PRODUCTIVITY METHOD

So, I suppose it's time to do some actual work now.

I've always had a complicated relationship with productivity. I consider myself to be a little lazy, and the more I think about it, the more I realise that I'm *lucky* to be that way. I can never pretend to be a perfectionist; I don't see the point in it. To me – and countless other people in the history of the productivity discourse – *done* is very much better than *perfect*. Despite my slight embarrassment at my tendency to put efficiency over perfection, it's a talent to know when something is more effort than it's worth: I know when to put an hour in, and when to put a month in. I know when to delegate, and when to turn my phone off and conceptualise a whole campaign in an hour because I know I'm the only one who can bring my vision to life. At the end of the day, my laziness is efficiency, and it's a huge part of why I've been able to do what I have. Genuinely. If you were to ask me what personality trait has helped me the most, my answer would be being a lazy workaholic: always ready to put the work in, but also always ready to stop that work, pass it on and move on to make room for more work.

Truth be told, I feel a little nervous going into this chapter. We've developed an overly delicate attitude towards self-care, and everyone is worried about being too direct. Suggest to someone that maybe they don't need to have a relaxing bath to feel better – maybe they need to finish the work and have a bath afterwards – and you'll be looked at as if you've just told them to cut off their own head. It stands true that sometimes we may not *want* to get work done but we *need* to, for our mental health if nothing else. There's a time for the bath and there's a time to suck it up and graft. (All this big scary talk is making me feel like the Gordon Ramsay of productivity, and I kind of like it. I won't be calling you an idiot sandwich, but you might be calling yourself one by the time you finish this chapter.)

This is the part of the book you need to read when you're being too soft on yourself to your own detriment – not when you're on the cusp of burnout. I hope to enable you to tell the difference and to allow you to have conviction around when you need to kick yourself up the ass, and when you need to unplug and be a potato on the sofa. These are the two sides to this book and you need to be able to navigate between them.

The plain truth is that we all need to work, and we're better off working *smart*. Working smart – being productive, efficient and

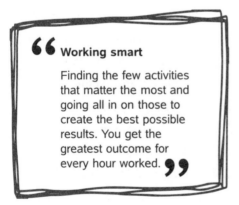

❝ Working smart

Finding the few activities that matter the most and going all in on those to create the best possible results. You get the greatest outcome for every hour worked. ❞

effective – means that we're going to have more time to do more of what we love, whether that's more work or more play. That being said, I don't buy into the whole, almost cult-like, 'work smart so you don't have to work hard' rhetoric. Working smart *is* hard. It requires a lot of time spent getting to know yourself, and a good dose of tough love. On top of that, it's something that will evolve throughout your working life. It seems unfair to create the expectation that, once we've learnt to work smart, it's all smooth sailing. We all want different things – whether that's an early retirement, Tim Ferriss's 4-hour work week, a job we love wholeheartedly, or a promotion – and all those things will require at least some periods of head down, *this is really shit and I'd rather be out with my friends* work. Every single goal you want to achieve will require those moments – even if you're about to go and live in a treehouse and sustenance farm for your food. (Have you ever tried to grow an aubergine? That shit is *hard*.)

Over the past year, I've realised that the way society *sees* work has had a huge impact on *how* I work. When I first realised I was altering the way I operated based on this work-sharing culture, I started to see 'announcement culture' everywhere I looked. Yet as I tried to research further, I was unable to find any developed discussion on the phenomenon. The way I see it, announcement culture is our ever-growing need to announce everything we're doing, therefore perpetuating our anxiety of having 'things' to announce in the first place. This includes working towards 'announceable' goals and judging our success and that of others on the quantity (rather than the quality) of announcements made. It's the reason, I realised, for my personal and undeniable love of ticking things off, regardless of whether it was actually useful work. The gratification I received from being able to see just how much I'd ticked off far outweighed the reality that I wasn't making proper, effective progress. Sure, maybe at times it spurred on further productivity by boosting my self-belief that I could get things done, but if I'm being honest, it was largely a procrastination cover-up.

At one point, I lived off the recognition I received for my work ethic. (Who am I kidding, I'm definitely still unlearning this.) I concentrated on 'acting' like an entrepreneur, 'acting' like a CEO, doing things I could shout about, hours I could prove I'd worked, to-do lists I could show off completed. My mile-long to-do list was reminiscent of that *tick tick tick*ing crocodile Captain Hook was afraid of. I was making progress in some ways, but was it *optimised*? Was it *actual* work that would take me somewhere next week? Next year? Not really, no. The validation we get from considering something 'done', combined with our need for instant gratification, means that we often prioritise easy work over actual progress. Our quest for announceable 'productivity' that we can show off (for self-worth and social media kudos) means we hold ourselves back from going beyond surface-level work and actually making profound progress. If you find yourself doing the same, you need to sack this view of productivity to build real foundations for your work and career, and gain genuine traction towards your goals. Let's get this straight: productivity ≠ ticking off your traditional to-do list. You have to have the *right* to-do list, filled with deep work, comprehensive tasks directed towards larger goals, and a number of quick boxes to tick.

> **❝ Deep work**
>
> As defined by computer scientist and professor Cal Newport, deep work is any 'professional activity performed in a state of distraction-free concentration that pushes your cognitive capabilities to their limit. These efforts create new value, improve your skill, and are hard to replicate.' **❞**

We're about to get into some real juicy productivity tips – but first we need to get comfortable with tough love. I could give you all the tips in the world, but if you're not honest with yourself, I might as well be speaking gibberish. It'll be a waste of time until you can give yourself the honesty you deserve. Just because most other people are never direct with us, it doesn't mean that we can beat around the bush internally. Perhaps in our (quintessentially British) indirectness, we've lost the ability to be sincere with ourselves. You're going to need honesty each and every day – on those days you want to work less and on those you want to work more. Are you sitting back and relaxing because you *need* it, or are you just putting off yet another half-done project? We can't listen to social media when it's telling us to both hu$tle and put on a facemask and cancel that meeting in the name of self-care: because it's not an objective choice. No one but you can tell which you need to do, so get honest and clear with yourself. It all comes down to truly knowing yourself: you need to understand your own strengths, boundaries, desires and downfalls.

How to manage your time

Learning how to manage your time is one of, if not the most crucial part of living a productive life. It allows you to structure your time in order to fit in everything you want and need to be doing, and is one of the most effective ways of reducing stress. When you can *feel* the stress tidal wave coming over you – you have 352 things floating around in your brain in no particular order, all of which are a top priority, and none of which make sense – you need to be able to know how to effectively write it all down and sort it out. Time management is a form of stress management: the key to success while simultaneously protecting your sanity.

In order to do manage your time successfully, you need a method – how to work out what to do first, where the important things go, *how to stay sane*. It needs to become second nature to you, so that the instant you start to feel that wave coming, you automatically step back and figure it out so you can surf it rather than be pulled under and get water up your nose. You know that saying: 'if you need something done, give it to the busiest person in the room'? That's largely true, but it means fuck-all unless that busy person is *efficiently* and *effectively* busy. I first learnt about the concept of efficiency vs effectiveness in Tim Ferriss's *The 4-Hour Work Week*. While I disagree with aspects of the book, this part was definitely important. There is significant scholarship out there on the topic, and it certainly rings true both in terms of boosting productivity and in considering the importance of that work being sustainable and directional above all else. Ferriss sums up the concept of effectiveness by giving it the succinct qualifier of 'doing the things that get you closer to your goals', alongside his description of efficiency: 'performing a given task (whether important or not) in the most economical manner possible'. The combination, then, is the winner. This is a huge part of how we learn the difference between busyness and productive, organised work.

The first rule of time management is prioritisation. The simple truth is that if you choose not to do something, *it is not a priority*. That's the first bit of tough love. Substitute saying, 'I don't have time' with 'it's not a priority', and you'll instantly get closer to the self-accountability needed for discipline and progress. Something not being a priority is *absolutely fine*: you just need to be able to acknowledge that. Trust me, I know this is a lot harder than it seems. Once you've understood that something hasn't been a priority, the next thing you need to decide is whether you're going to change that, or whether you're going to accept it. Both are acceptable, and tied to where you want to be next week, next month and next year.

Still not happy with not doing that thing you're not prioritising and need to accept isn't a priority? Change it! Make it a priority. Those are your two options – change it or accept it. If you're still falling short of your own expectations after that, it's your expectations that need to change rather than your priorities.

If you're struggling with working out what you should be doing, let alone when, I strongly recommend the Eisenhower Method. This focuses on differentiating between 'urgent' and 'important' tasks on your to-do list, so you can decide whether you need to do them, and if you do, how much of a priority they are compared to other tasks. This will help you to work out the content of your tasks (quadrants 1 and 2), and which you should be skipping altogether (quadrants 3 and 4). (Hint: these may be your favourite ones to procrastinate with.)

URGENT	IMPORTANT
① **DO FIRST** Your first tasks should be the ones that are both important and need to be finished that day.	② **SCHEDULE** If something is important but doesn't need to happen urgently, you should schedule it in to be done another time.
③ **DELEGATE** If it's an urgent but less important task, delegate it to others.	④ **DON'T DO** Tasks that are neither urgent nor important most likely don't need to be done at all.

It's not a complicated method, and it should definitely help with the basic principles of working out what's worth your time, both now and later. I personally find that I automatically do the 'urgent-important' classification in my head. In my opinion, this alone is not organisational enough beyond deciphering what you should and shouldn't do, but it's a great first step.

Once you've got your tasks figured out, in order to prioritise, you need to organise. I don't want to toot my own horn, but *toot toot*: I'm *great* at organisation. Running two businesses while completing university and attempting to have a somewhat functioning social life (and stay sane), has meant I've definitely gained my 10,000 hours of time-management practice. I wouldn't consider myself an expert at most things (even those I'm employed to do), but give me an impossible number of tasks, tell me I can't fit them all in, and watch me fly. It comes with pros and cons (*not* feeling organised gives me slight heart palpitations), but it's something I know is one of my strengths, and something I get asked about all the time. There's no one-size-fits-all approach, but this wouldn't be my book if I didn't impart my might-as-well-be-copyrighted organisational methods.

First things first, you'll notice my main principles are based around visibility and awareness – a clear sight of what you have to do is *essential* to tackling it effectively. No matter how overwhelming, your to-dos need to be visible or you cannot progress towards getting it all done.

STEP 1: Keep an electronic calendar

Seriously, this is your advice, Grace? What a waste of £16.99.

But really: we're in 2021 now, and we all know electronic calendars can remember things we'd forgotten we'd even booked. Even better, use whichever calendar is connected to your email server so it can sync up. There are so many out there, so try 'em out for yourself and find your perfect Cinderella-shoe-calendar fit. My email and calendar servers of choice are good old Google. Electronic calendars allow you to book years in advance and get alerts closer to the time, then you can move things around to your heart's content without your diary looking like a toddler's scribble book.

A second benefit is that you can create different calendars for different areas of your work and keep your social life separate, which can be really helpful in cultivating that work-life balance we'll be discussing later on. Separating things visually goes a long way in giving you peace of mind.

STEP 2: Keep a paper diary too

Don't worry, the calendar obsession stops after this point.

I *highly* recommend that your paper diary has a double-spread full-week view so you can visualise the entire week as a whole. On Sunday evening or Monday morning, before starting work, transfer everything from your electronic calendar to your paper diary. I know this sounds crazy and very time consuming, but it really isn't – especially if you think how much time you'll save from being stressed and overwhelmed by letting your subconscious mind mull your week over before it's even started. It's not about just duplicating calendars, it's a small task that will give you the birds-eye view you need to effectively manage your workload, even when things change last-minute. Visibility is the first step in making this all work, and the negligible time it takes to do this is nothing in the face of the benefit it will provide.

STEP 3: The to-do-table method

Here's where it gets really good and practical. The to-do list is *so* last generation: we're all about the to-do *table* now. This is what will help you to organise the things you *do* need to be doing, following your clarification of what your to-dos entail by using the Eisenhower Method (see page 47).

This is a very serious question: why does your to-do list look like the Top 40 music chart, please? All your tasks are not the same: they are not of equal priority and they are certainly going to overwhelm the hell out of you when you look down and see 703 things you need to do by 5pm. My to-do table method is based on the essential principles of task batching, while allowing full visibility over our days. I make this table at the beginning of every single day, and it also includes items that aren't going to get done that day, for full visibility and order. It will take you five minutes and save you way more than that by allowing you to prioritise, visualise and group tasks all in one before you even consider getting down to it. Although this might feel like a whole load of fancy paperwork, you honestly do not have a chance of remaining organised and calm under a heavy workload, getting everything done on time *and* fitting in your lower priority 'wants' (like the gym, seeing friends, going on a walk), if you can't spend five minutes getting your head in the game.

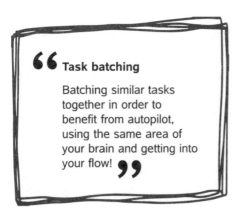

" Task batching

Batching similar tasks together in order to benefit from autopilot, using the same area of your brain and getting into your flow! **"**

Your to-do table (TDT) is going to look a little something like this:

Quick Ticks	Tasks	Projects

Quick Ticks: Things that will take five minutes or less.

- Examples: 'respond to work Whatsapps', 'upload announcement to Instagram story', 'send message to colleague about office party'.

Tasks: Things that will take you up to thirty minutes. These will require some work and headspace, but don't involve more than two or three mini tasks to get the whole task done.

- Examples: 'compose email to product team about sustainable fashion article', 'draft response to lawyer', 'review app development presentation'.

Projects: These are the big boys. They may not be for today, but you still want to be conscious of them as you go through your day and carry them over into your week.

- Examples: 'design new collection', 'prepare full market research of competitors', 'prepare presentation on financials'.

These will then be broken down into tasks when you confront them in time blocks. For example, 'design new collection' could be split into the following:

- Perform seasonal trend research on WGSN
- Create moodboard for collection

- Decipher how many pieces the collection needs
- Roughly design pieces
- Write up spec descriptions
- Send to product team for review

Top tip: when you know you're going to be doing a project in a particular week, split the project into tasks when you're doing your first TDT of the week. That way, you can identify whether you need something from someone else to start, and get yourself clear on how many time blocks you need to finish the whole project.

STEP 4: Slot them in

Once you've created your TDT, choose the Quick Ticks, Tasks and Projects you need to do that day before you start work (that means at 8.45am latest if you have a 9am call). Have a look at your day in your calendar, and slot the day's worth of tasks in between fixed commitments. (Remember, a great time to blitz those Quick Ticks is those awkward fifteen minutes between calls.) To slot everything in, I use a technique called *time-blocking*.

I didn't invent the concept of time-blocking, but honestly, with the amount of enthusiasm I have for it you'd think Ms Time-Block paid my salary. My life is #ad-sponsored by time-blocking. The amount of freedom you have to time-block is totally dependent on what you do for work, if you're a freelancer, how far you are in your career, whether you're at uni … the list goes on. But whether you're using this as the core of your organisational week or just to make the most of your evenings and weekends to spur on your side-hustle, time-blocking is *superior*.

Time-blocking

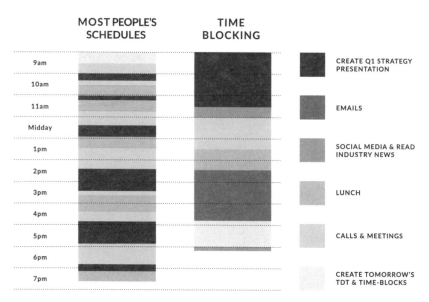

Task-batching + Preparation = Time-blocking

The concept is simple: as much as you can, divide your day into blocks of time and dedicate each block to accomplishing a specific task or group of tasks. If you have no control at all over your calls and they're littered throughout your days, the time around fixed commitments should still be time-blocked. When you look at your day or week in advance, decipher where you are left with chunks of time to fill. Then, add a time-block to your diary as if it's an appointment or meeting (which it is: with yourself). This might require you to shift your lunch break or start working a bit earlier, but ideally 1–1.5-hour time blocks are about right to confront your batched tasks or projects. If you have greater freedom with your calendar, base your week around these time-blocks. For example, I currently have

Tuesday afternoons, Wednesday full-days and Thursday afternoons blocked out for writing this book.

The best way to perfect the use of time-blocks is to know yourself and your working habits. Are you most creative in the morning? I know I am, so I try to block out mornings to conceptualise for my businesses or jot down ideas for this book. It's all about 'learning' yourself and how your mind works, and using that to create an organised life around any fixed commitments you have. Your own work should have as much priority – if not more, although I know that's not always possible – as fixed work commitments, and planting *your* goals into your calendar is the first step in making them happen. You have to be able to visualise the progress you can make in your day and your week, or you won't have the *space* to make that progress.

An unfortunate reality is that sometimes time-blocking has to go out the window with the rest of your schedule when unexpected, urgent work pops up. Time-blocking hugely increases productivity and efficiency, however, so you're always going to have more time for those extra tasks if you time-block well, regardless of how unexpected they are. It also means the majority of your top-priority work will be out of the way before these things pop up, as chances are they appear later on in the day. This method will help you use your time wisely and productively, but that doesn't mean other people will, or that the universe is going to time-block according to your plans. You have to be adaptable and get whatever has popped up done as quickly and thoroughly as possible. We can't always account for the unforeseen, but we can account for our reactions. If you've been productively working through your week, you'll be in a much stronger position to tackle whatever the world throws your way. The beauty of being human is that we don't short-circuit when something doesn't go according to our rigid plans – we make space for that flexibility. And if you find it happening more often than you'd like, or panicking when it does, I'd recommend scheduling in some 'unexpected work' time-blocks into your day. That way, you have allocated time for these drop-in tasks should they arise – and if nothing comes up, you've just gained some extra time in your day!

I want to caveat this by saying that my methods aren't going to work for everyone. There's so much information out there to improve your time-management and organisation, so don't use this as a bible. That being said, I really want you to at least try these suggestions, and tweak them as you learn what works for you – whether that's adding more columns to your TDT or writing your paper diary out on a computer rather than the other way around. *You* are what matters here. And even once you've worked out your own methods and variations, the reality is you'll still have off days and weeks. And that's okay. I truly believe that as long as you know what works for you and you're honest about where to apply it, you're on the path to productive and mindful success.

Deep work

To take your time-blocking to the next level, I want to introduce deep work back into the conversation. We touched on it very briefly earlier, but as any Cal Newport diehard will know, a little is not enough.

Deep work is all about accepting that we will be bombarded from all sides by notifications and instant distractions, and that it's our job to combat that and protect our space when we need to. In other words, it's all about changing the way you work, setting deep work slots (aligned with time-blocks) and concentrating fully on your work during those times. No distractions allowed. Sure, you can be the quickest text-replier ever, but surely you'd rather get shit done so that you have all the time in the world later to make a meme or tackle your emails (in their designated time-block)? The more efficient you are, the more time you can spend doing literally *whatever* else you want to. Stop allowing instant gratification to get the better of you – *you are better than that.*

All right, Grace Ramsay, back to the concept.

Deep work fits squarely within the realms of our time-blocking conversations, and how to use time-blocks effectively. Where Newport's deep work can be actioned directly within time-blocking is the contrast between deep and shallow work. Shallow work, as opposed to deep work, is categorised by 'non-cognitively demanding, logistical-style tasks'. *Ding ding,* is that the admin bell I hear? You need to ask yourself which time-blocks you will dedicate to one or the other, and make sure you're scheduling and performing them accordingly. There is no benefit to batching your tasks together if they differ between the two working styles. Absorb yourself in your deep work and batch together your shallow work so it doesn't take over your days.

Deep work means that we can take our valuable time-blocks, and make them more than just good planning. It means that we can actually get the job done efficiently and with the quality required. You can time-block every hour until you retire, but unless you use those blocks wisely and without distraction, you'll be hard-pressed to find any other benefit than your schedule looking nice and busy.

Getting into deep work might be a struggle for you, especially if it's not a task that you'd qualify as a micro-passion and therefore gets you into your flow (see pages 33 and 77). My personal stages of deep work go a little like this:

DEEP WORK STAGES

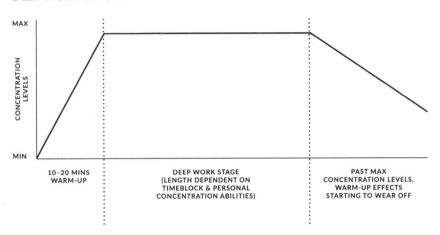

The warm-up is the most crucial part, and if you're not passionate about the task at hand, this can be especially difficult (and therefore especially important). You need to get yourself in the zone to be as productive as possible during the majority of your deep work session. Sure, you can jump straight into the task – the majority of concentration comes from discipline after all – but just like any sport, it's good to limber up first. Personally, I find it makes the quality of the work better and I am able to concentrate for longer. I like to use deep work triggers to get me going. Try mine, tweak them, learn yours, and get going.

I recommend focusing on related tasks if you're coming from a similar type of work, as they're going to get you in the zone quicker. Related tasks can be linked in any number of ways. If you're writing an article on renewable energy, for example, you could trigger deep work by either starting to write

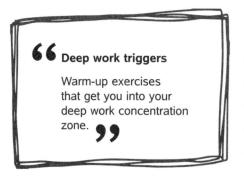

❝ Deep work triggers

Warm-up exercises that get you into your deep work concentration zone. ❞

anything to get yourself into the writing zone, or by reading an article or watching a YouTube video on the subject for inspiration. For me, I do one or more of the following for ten or twenty minutes, then hop straight into my deep work:

1. **Read a related article or blog.** Whatever the task, reading an article on the topic gets me into the zone straight away. I find blogs are especially accessible; blogs and articles are short and sweet, and have the added bonus of not having the temptation to read on. Whatever you do though, set yourself a time limit for doing this. You may find numerous interesting articles, and if you don't have clear parameters of when to move on, we all know you'll just end up down a rabbit hole. Discipline is key!

2. **Write down my current thoughts.** If your task is writing a newsletter, jot down a few unfiltered sentences on the subject before allowing yourself to dive into the actual process of writing the full thing. Chuck perfectionism out the window; these first sentences don't need to be perfect or even used in the end – just write!

3. **Set intentions.** Write down your goals for the deep work session, clearly and concisely, in bite-sized chunks. Set small goals that lead to the ultimate aim of the session, then get going.

If you're coming from a completely unrelated task – like speaking or presenting before going into writing – you'll need to bring yourself back down to earth first. A bit like a palate cleanser between courses at a fancy tasting restaurant. Try something that gets you concentrated, whether or not it's related to what you want to throw yourself into, then move closer to the subject with an article or something similar. The way I see it is like this.

COMING FROM A SIMILAR ACTIVITY

COMING FROM A COMPLETELY DIFFERENT TASK

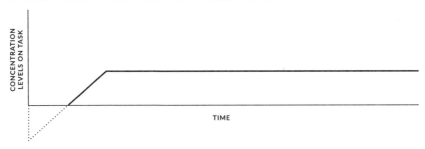

On the opposite end of the spectrum to deep work is admin. We all know admin work is a bottomless pit that will swallow your time quicker than you can drunk-eat a Domino's pizza. It's an inevitable part of any job, especially if you are a student, just starting out, or working in a small business, but it should not be given any more priority than just being a necessary evil. It's the enemy of true progress: it'll make you feel accomplished (*tick tick tick*), but really it's a black hole for your time.

These are my three rules when it comes to combating the admin demon, waiting in the shadows to zap your time and creativity:

- **Don't start the day with admin.** I cannot stress this enough. Never. Start. The. Day. With. Admin. By the time you've finished, it'll be 2pm and your creativity will have gone back to bed for a siesta. I know you mean well, and I know you're just trying to get the boring things out of the way, but what will end up happening is that you'll feel a whole load of validation for ticking off things that didn't require much brainpower and could have waited till later in the day, and then struggle to get into any deep work and make real progress.

- **Set an email alarm.** Time-block email checking into your day (limit it to two or three times), and turn off notifications. You might no longer win the prize for quickest response, but 1 guarantee your work will be of much higher quality, and that's what really matters. (Obviously please ignore this point if your job focuses around responding to emails. You will still benefit from time-blocking them around other tasks, but first and foremost please make sure you're doing your job!)

- **Delegate.** This is particularly important for anyone self-employed, but is relevant beyond that too. As a rule of thumb, if you are self-employed and able to hire extra help, you should be spending time doing things that only *you* can do. Aside from this, delegation can and should work as part of any team, and according to pretty much all modern economics, dividing labour into specialties is certainly the way to create the best, most efficient work possible. It's clear that some people – myself included – are scared of delegation, and it's natural to want to own the whole task, but understanding your strengths and those of your team, and trusting the people you work with, is key. You might be best delegating certain tasks to someone better or more efficient than you within your team, and picking up the slack elsewhere for them.

Making even the most productive people more productive

Maybe you already do some of the things I've mentioned, maybe you have your own methods and already consider yourself pretty productive, or maybe you don't work in a job where those tips are applicable – so if you're looking to become a master of optimising your time, here are some universal rules for making even the most productive people more productive:

1. **Be aware of how long tasks *actually* take you.** You'll find it very hard to plan effectively if your estimates are off. Spend a week or so monitoring and taking note of how long it takes you to compose a simple email or complete a longer project, and you'll be much more in touch with your working processes and capabilities in no time.

2. **Take breaks.** This is where I often fall down – when I'm in my flow, I'll work on something for hours until I've exhausted all my energy and then find it impossible to focus for the rest of the day. This might be the only option when working close to a deadline, but it shouldn't be a regular occurrence. There's all sorts of research out there on how long you should work for in one go, but I think it totally depends on the type of work, how much focus it requires, and your personal working preferences. Consider the following to discover your optimum working time:

o How long does it take you to lose concentration on a task?

o Be aware of the fact that you'll be able to concentrate on some tasks longer than others, so categorise the three sections of your TDT into time limits. For instance, I can work on projects for about two hours productively, but quick ticks lose me after about forty minutes tops, with tasks sitting in the middle at about 1–1.5 hours. Time-block according to these limits as much as you can.

o Sometimes you won't be able to concentrate for as long as your regular allocations – if you're tired, burned out, or even just hungover. Take a break if you can. If not, shorten your blocks for the day and take regular invigorating breaks; just focus extra hard on not getting distracted in those breaks or falling asleep unintentionally.

3. **Take weekends.** Making a habit of working mindlessly through weekends because you 'haven't done enough' during the week will just get you into a rut, constantly chasing your tail and never resting enough. Stretch your hours all you want in the week, but make non-negotiable non-work time for yourself each weekend. You can't pour from an empty cup.

4. **Make your own deadlines.** Having twenty-three things due on the same day is a recipe for overwhelm, but just because they're all due on one day, it absolutely does not mean you should be aiming to complete them all on that one date. Preparation is the key here. Set deadlines according to your time-blocking, giving yourself a realistic amount of time to complete the tasks (see point 1). *The* deadline is not *your* deadline. As soon as you ace this, you'll be much further along to being able to balance the fun stuff too. At university I was very partial to setting intense

personal deadlines so that I could have a hungover morning when I'd otherwise have to be working. It's all about give and take. Student work alchemy!

5.   **Tidy your work space.** Make it as nice as possible, with plants, clean surfaces, ordered documents. You'll be surprised how much of a difference it makes to your focus.

6.   **The two-minute rule.** Entrepreneur Steve Olenski recommends this as his key productivity tip: if you see a task or action that you know can be done in two minutes or less, do it immediately. And I agree – to an extent. It can be a slippery slope to Admin Demon, so make sure you have the discipline to understand that doing four two-minute tasks is not the same as just doing one, and if you're in the creative flow and something pops up – don't do it!

  o   According to a study by the University of California Irvine, it takes on average twenty-three minutes and fifteen seconds to get yourself back on track following an interruption. Just think how much that can add up with emails and poor decisions during the day. I don't know about you, but I'd rather take an extra lunch hour than lose that much time to 'quickly do something'.

7.   **Hold and engage in effective meetings.** Meetings can be an absolute drain on effective time use. I recommend planning ahead of time to make sure you get the most out of them in the least amount of time: write down your questions beforehand, and make sure there's an agenda (of sorts) in place. It goes without saying that some meetings could be an email, so try not to be that person who schedules them just to look official when it's not the most productive option. And concentrate! We all use meetings as

catch-up sessions for admin a little too much: if you're there, be present. I'm a huge proponent for meetings being a phone and laptop-free zone – there are minimal interruptions or distractions, and it keeps the meeting focused.

8. **Use focus-enhancing apps.** There are so many to choose from: on your phone, desktop plug-ins, newsfeed blockers. My favourite is the mobile app *Forest*. You grow a virtual tree for a set amount of time and can't go on your phone during that time. This app single-handedly improved my studying for university finals tenfold, and it's a fantastic way of policing your time-blocking. If you're competitive, add your friends on the app and let the focus tree-growing Olympics commence. I also thoroughly recommend a newsfeed blocker for your laptop. Save mindless scrolling for hangovers and lazy mornings: your work time is the time to actually make moves, so you can do what you want later.

9. **Turn off notifications.** You might check your apps a little more when you first turn off notifications to see if that person you went on a date with has texted back yet, but in time you'll find yourself checking them less and less. This isn't always possible, of course. If your boss expects you to always be on call, please don't mute her and blame me. How about putting on an Out-of-Office alert telling people you're focusing on offline work? This works especially well when working remotely as people can't physically see you're focusing when they interrupt you. It'll work miracles for your concentration, and remember that communication is key. I know it's not always possible, but being transparent with your team about how this helps you focus should be enough. As the world moves further away from

emails and towards instant messaging, you need to set boundaries where you can. Similarly, offices come with a huge amount of distractions – from phones ringing to colleagues popping over to say hello. Every office will have different capabilities, but you could turn your in-person distractions off by booking a meeting room to work in or heading down to the café next door to concentrate on deeper work.

10. **Commit to tasks.** Commit to the task you're doing rather than multi-task and you'll get it done in half the time.

11. **Listen to your honest self.** Will listening to booming music help this work session, or will it slow you down? I'm not making a judgement call either way, but you need to decide what you want from your session. I feel like I'm beating the same drum, but try to make your work about work. Get it done efficiently and allow more time for doing what you want.

12. **Set intentions for the day.** Why not try setting your intentions for the day to warm up your brain when you begin work? I like to keep these separate from my TDT, and have them centre around my mindset. Examples include:

     o I will not allow myself to get overwhelmed after my call with the operations team.
     o I will cook myself a delicious, nutritious lunch.
     o I will build five hours of 'focus trees' today.

13. **Strengthen your strengths.** Pareto's Principle says that roughly 80 per cent of results come from 20 per cent of causes. Make your 20 per cent the best it can be and watch your results skyrocket. Some of my favourite ways of doing this are also the cheapest: reading

> **"Pareto's Principle**
>
> The principle was largely made popular by Richard Koch's book *The 80/20 Principle*, in which he describes it as the rule that '80 per cent of results flow from 20 per cent of causes'. What that means, he argues, is that 'you can achieve much more with much less effort, time and resources, simply by concentrating on the all-important 20 per cent'. The theory certainly has its limits – dropping 80 per cent of your work immediately for your favourite 20 per cent will hardly do you many favours – but the sentiment that you should focus and enhance your strengths is definitely a useful one. **"**

articles and studies, reading books and watching YouTube videos. You don't need a degree to become knowledgeable on a subject. Remember too that the best way to get good at something is by practising it!

14. **Say no.** Practise saying no to meetings, lunches and new projects that wouldn't be the best use of your time right now. Of course, your ability and confidence to do this will improve as you gain more freedom in your work, but as a general rule, look out for yourself and your capacity. Normalise saying no. This is a struggle, no matter what stage of your career you're at, but it's so important. If you work within a traditional structure, talk to your manager about your workload – the more awareness they have, the more they can speak up for you, and even say no for you when needed or when more senior people throw their weight around. You may not feel like you can – it does depend on your relationship to a

degree – but part of their job is to look after your workload. Once again, communication is key!

15. **Tasks vs time.** Work by task rather than time where possible. Clock-watching is boring as hell and a waste of your time, as well as everyone else's. Understand how much capacity you have and work on tasks accordingly. Finding it hard to concentrate? Set yourself a few easier tasks to complete and promise yourself a break. Make sure this is a set amount though – don't fall into the Admin Demon's trap! If this doesn't work, take an invigorating break (star jumps get my vote), give yourself a pep talk, or call it a day if that's what you really need (and have the ability) to do.

16. **Advance-TDTs.** Do your TDT at the end of the day for the following day, so you have full visibility of what tomorrow will look like. This will also help you to switch off easier in the evening, because you've written it all down and don't have to hold it in your head or worry about what tomorrow might bring. Don't go in blind – visibility is key!

17. **Use your commute ...** to get your head in the game! (All right, *High School Musical*.) Use it as a warm-up for the rest of your day: listen to podcasts you find inspiring, read over your TDT, prepare questions for your meetings, read a book. It doesn't matter how long or short your commute is, it'll add up big time in the long run, and getting into the right mindset is the most important part here.

   o The caveat is that this is the 'working hard' version of this tip; there is a 'hardly working' version too. Sometimes, what you really need is to use your commute to chill out and for that to be a time that you enjoy. While the above can certainly increase productivity and helps you arrive to work already in the zone, when I'm overworked I like to use my commute in the opposite way – slowing down a bit to walk, buying myself a yummy treat, talking to a friend on the phone. As always, it depends on what you really need.

18. **Exercise.** Work some form of exercise into your week, and make it one that you love! You won't stick to it if you don't enjoy it – and I would know, I built a whole business around that idea. We all know that working out is great for our mental and physical health, but it's following through that's difficult. I work out every weekday morning for twenty minutes, doing whatever I fancy that day (usually weightlifting or interval training cardio), and I cannot tell you how much moving my body gets my brain going.

19. **Eat well and stay hydrated.** Understand that you're feeding your brain and not just your body. Learn which foods help and which hinder your concentration. Fun fact about me: I can't concentrate if I eat a load of onions in my lunch. Knowing this is good for my focus (and for anyone close enough to smell my breath). Staying hydrated also often forces you up from your seat, which can help you avoid feeling lethargic from not moving all day – this is especially important when working from home.

20. **Just start!** Feeling unproductive? Can't get creative? Don't know how to start? The answer is ... just start! Put down your phone and write something. Stop complaining that you feel uninspired while your thumb is mindlessly running a marathon down your screen. It doesn't matter what you write – the important thing is getting your brain warmed up.

Create a routine that works for you

The amount of structure we each need in our lives is totally subjective, but I am strongly of the opinion that we all need a little more than we think we do. This isn't to say that we need rigid, school-esque timetables – I'm not about to tell you to schedule your day by the minute, or to time your coffee breaks – but rather, that we can all benefit from following a routine around a set of rules that are true to how we work and live best. Developing a routine is all about working out what works for you.

Granted, if you're a freelancer, you'll have a great deal more freedom than if you're just starting out at a corporate job – but the important thing to remember is that the new working world is often a lot more flexible than you think. I think our schooling system makes us think the working world will be rigid and inflexible, and makes us resent that structure. Most likely, your boss just wants you to work the best you possibly can – it makes them look better and gets results – and it's up to you to suss how much of your own routine can be applied to your job. This may involve asking your supervisor whether you can be in the office on an 8am to 4pm schedule because you like getting things done before the morning starts, or your creativity is dulled as soon as the office is noisy. If you don't ask, you don't get! Just remember to be professional, and that some people – especially older or conversely less experienced managers wanting to assert themselves – can be resistant to change. Prove yourself and work hard – the more you do this, the more trust and freedom you'll likely earn.

I have a little formula when it comes to creating my routine. I know I promised no school timetables, but when explaining to a friend how I created my own evolving and adaptable routine back at university, this maths lesson was the only thing that made sense among my ramblings:

Rituals + Habits = Overall Routine

Rituals are concepts and rules that you consciously follow throughout your routine, facilitated by discipline. An example could be a quick yoga flow or full body stretch in the morning. You make an active decision to set your alarm ten minutes earlier, so that you have this time to yourself.

Habits are subconscious actions we regularly perform. For example, getting up at 6am and going through your autopilot of showering, washing your face and getting dressed because it's just what you do.

Our **Overall Routine** is the result of adding these two elements together – it's not a set schedule, but an accumulation of habits and rituals, which you can then apply to how you deal with other commitments.

Over time, rituals can become habits, and that's where we really start to see the difference. Habits are a sort of back-up engine that kicks in when we need it. They're the safety net of motivation. The truth is, motivation isn't going to be there the whole time. It's not going to be there when you drag yourself out of bed for a 5km run – the only thing that can help you there is the discipline needed to make it a ritual, or a habit if you've got that far down the line. In reality, we don't always operate at our optimum, and discipline and habit are going to fill that gap. You *need* good habits to form a good routine that keeps you productive *and* happy, rather than driving on empty.

So, how do we create good rituals and habits?

I absolutely love James Clear's book, *Atomic Habits*, which affirms the idea that habits (tiny changes) can and will change your entire life. He argues that we don't need to think big, we need to think *small*, and I couldn't agree more. Our habits are what define us; they're what we do again and again, adding together to form a routine that dictates our life's trajectory. I won't restate his whole book – I'd really recommend reading it – but essentially, it's in the small things that change really happens. Create rituals, transform them into habits, and use these as the rules on which to create your routine.

When I look at my own habits, I have the tendency to think of myself as a machine that *should* be able to fix its mechanical nicks. Clear talks a lot about this feeling, and how to combat it, in his theory of 'The Plateau of Latent Potential': the idea that we expect our habit change trajectory to be a steep upwards arrow, when in reality change is slow and often disappointing at first, which is why so many people give up. It's only when we push through this 'plateau' that we become 'an overnight success'. All the same, I find this sense of failure really hard to get through, and this is where I believe rituals come in, to make the process of creating new habits a lot friendlier to human nature. I introduce rituals to my routine to make it better, while knowing that they might never become habits. I try to wake up ten minutes before I need to because, after years of last-minute wake-ups, I've realised that ten minutes of waking mindfulness is a lot more relaxing than ten minutes of extra sleep – but this will always be down to me making a decision to set that alarm earlier. Other rituals I have include loose 'rules', like working on the hardest task I have first to get it over and done with. This isn't yet a habit, and it might never become one because it doesn't need to happen every day and it's too conceptual to become a concrete habit, but it's a rule of thumb to boost my productivity. I recommend basing your rituals on your working preferences and whatever you know helps you to work best.

You might be reading this and thinking you have no idea what works for you, and that's the whole fun of it. Okay, I know that having 'routine', 'work' and 'fun' in the same sentence may seem contradictory, but hear me out. The most important thing to remember is that your rituals, like everything else, will evolve as your skills, priorities and preferences change throughout your life. It's your duty to address how and when these change, and alter your routine accordingly. Your rituals might change with the season, or as a result of events in your life. You might be bursting at the seams with creativity at 5am in the summer when the sun is up, but the thought of starting the day before 8am in the winter might make you want to vomit. In a period full of evening events, mornings may be harder as you go to bed late. Learning your rituals is all about being adaptable and *knowing yourself* (are you starting to spot a trend here?). But try not to fall into the trap of becoming stubborn with your rituals, because if you have any contact with the outside world, things are going to come up, urgent projects will land on your desk, and you're going to have to relinquish control.

If anything, having rituals in place for these situations can help you navigate through them. For example, if a crisis pops up when I'm about to clock off for the day, I have my rituals in place. I hop straight on a call with the team involved, let them fill me in and we write up a potential plan of action. I send a provisional 'I might have to cancel, don't hate me pls' message to my friends if I had plans, I make myself a nice drink (it doesn't have to be alcoholic – sort of depends on the intensity of the crisis, to be honest), and put some music on. I might even order myself takeout. My working practices adapt from what they'd usually be for optimal *productivity*, to a more sympathetic 'sorry you're still working when you shouldn't be, from me, to me' for optimal *sanity*.

**VERY IMPORTANT CRISIS MANAGEMENT TO
DRINKING RELATIONSHIP GRAPH**

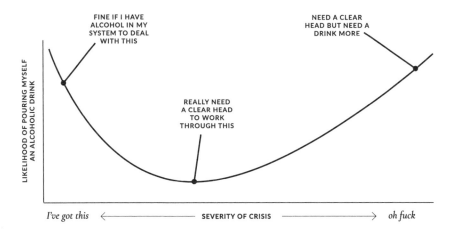

So, how do you establish your rituals?

The recipe for finding which rituals work for you is similar to discovering how you self-actualise. Take what you like and dislike, and add a large tablespoonful of where you want to be. So, if you like lying in bed till 2pm and then going out to dinner as the clock strikes 6pm, you're not going to want to make these your rituals if you also want your routine to be progress-filled and productive.

Ask yourself the following:

- Which morning routine makes you feel calmest and most equipped for the day ahead?
- When are you most productive in the day?
- Which of your working habits makes you feel most anxious?
- When do you find it hard to generate quality work?
- What do you wish you had time to do?

- What do you need to change in your daily life in order to reach your goals for the year?

Analyse how your work affects you and how you affect your work, and do more of what makes you happy and productive and less of what doesn't – most of the time it really is as simple as that. Take it gradually, pay close attention to when you feel most and least productive, create rituals that reflect those truths, and allow your routine to form around those rituals. You deserve your routine to be exactly that – *yours* – and you're the only person who can make it that way. We're brought up with rigid routines based around what works for other people, but at some point we need to bring that back to ourselves, or we can't expect to live a life with our goals and preferences at the centre.

*

Now, you can take all the techniques listed in this chapter and be the ultimate productivity guru, but it counts for nothing if you aren't producing *good* work. No matter your job or stage in your career, there are some practices that always ring true. I want to leave you with these tips before we move on.

- **Use spell check.** I ask every single person who works at my companies to use Grammarly. It's life-changing and saves so much time that I genuinely cannot understand why anyone wouldn't use it. It even corrects your tone of voice to be in line with your desired level of formality. Wow4technology. Good grammar or spelling are often taken for granted, but can be hard and time-consuming, especially if you're dyslexic or if English isn't your first language, but there are lots of tools out there to help you ace it.

- **Ask for help and/or clarification.** If you're unsure, ask! We all have the same goal – of producing the best work possible – and the hierarchy at the office is often less serious than it seems. You're much better clarifying something at the beginning of a project than having to redo it later.

- **Self-learn.** Make an effort to be better at your job, especially in areas you enjoy. It will make everyone's life easier, including yours! Try following relevant social media accounts in areas you'd like to learn more about. That way, even when you're running the thumb marathon, you'll be learning too.

- **Hone your craft.** Develop your strengths, even in weird and wonderful ways. There's no limit to how many strings you can add to your bow – improve in areas you're interested in, and make an effort to go above and beyond what is expected of you, especially when you enjoy it. That is one of the best ways of self-actualising.

- **Be polite.** In *and* out of work. Misunderstandings are common and everyone has bad days; communication is key, but it can often be hard to interpret tone over email or online. Take a breath and react with grace (not literally me, please, I don't want the drama).

- **Cultivate relationships.** Understand that everyone, even your horrible boss, is a human being with insecurities, flaws and downfalls. Make an effort to understand things from other people's perspectives and form relationships with people you wouldn't usually. Not only is it a nicer day-to-day experience, but it'll also mean that you can work with them more cohesively and produce better work together.

- **Don't be late.** Being late is not a personality trait; it's being disrespectful of others' time, and your own.

- **Think.** Critically, and outside of the box, more than you're expected to. Make wild suggestions, play devil's advocate in the workplace: if an idea can't stand up against criticism before it has even left the office, it's unlikely to fare well in the outside world. It's not easy, but people will appreciate you for doing it, I can guarantee that.

- **Be bold.** Ask for what you want. Be polite, yes, but still ask. If you don't ask, you don't get.

- **Be proactive.** Make the lives of the people around you easier. Do things without being asked, learn where problems regularly crop up, and plan in advance. Proactivity and taking the initiative will take you far.

- **Make an effort.** In your role and with the people around you. You can drift through on the bare minimum, but it'll only ever get you exactly that: the bare minimum.

CHAPTER THREE

LET IT FLOW

We've spent the last chapter talking about how to get stuff done, and that's all well and good, but now I want to talk about how to make it actually enjoyable so that your work itself – not just its products (reaching your goals, achievements and 'getting things done') – add to your life. If you think about it, the enjoyment we get from being engrossed in our work is where productivity feels most like self-care. While the conversation around productivity naturally obsesses on output – how to achieve more and achieve it quickly – the journey is equally, if not more important, so let's enjoy the process. After all, even if you have that hard-on-yourself tendency to count your productivity and work above your wellbeing, the more you enjoy something, the better your quality of work and life will be. Enjoying your work isn't over-indulgent, it's a win-win. Never forget that.

In our output-obsessed era, it's easy to fall into the trap of doing things quickly simply to get as much done as physically possible and to feel like we're progressing. This is especially true at the beginning of our careers. More and more, we tend to burn the candle at both ends, and though you

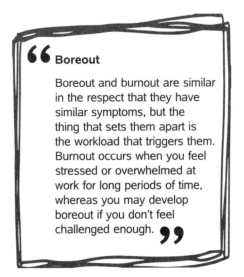

❝ Boreout

Boreout and burnout are similar in the respect that they have similar symptoms, but the thing that sets them apart is the workload that triggers them. Burnout occurs when you feel stressed or overwhelmed at work for long periods of time, whereas you may develop boreout if you don't feel challenged enough. ❞

might be able to fit as much into the first five years of your working life as possible, nothing can be productive in the long term if it's not sustainable. The reality is that we're going to be working for a while, and not all work is created equal. Some exists under the 'done is better than perfect' bubble, while some deserves more time and effort, if only because you enjoy doing it and it helps you to self-actualise. We're constantly balancing on a line between burnout and its lesser-known cousin, boreout. The causes might be polar opposites, but their symptoms are the same, as is the way to avoid them: enjoying your work by being careful in *how* you work.

Enjoying the work we do is, as we know, not just about doing something we love all the time. That would be amazing, wouldn't it! Yet the reality of the working world is far more complex than that. You could do something you 'love', and go through stages of strongly disliking your job – in fact, it would be strange not to. Or you could be doing something that you don't generally feel passionate about, but be intent on filling your day with micro-passions, building a happy, fulfilling and productive working life. The difference is what *you* fit into your day.

Of course, there's a huge element of privilege and variation in how much we're individually able to work micro-passions into our lives – what stage we are at in our careers, what our family situation looks like, how many jobs we're balancing, who we work for, what we do – and I can imagine it sounds quite rich coming from me, as someone leading organisations that I can shape around myself. But everything is relative, and while you can concentrate on things out of your control if you'd like to, it's likely to do you a disservice in the long run. And that's tough love coming from someone who *never* wants to offend people, even slightly. There'll always be people with more flexibility than you, and there'll always be people with less. We all have different circumstances, and as a result, productivity is more of a sliding scale – how we can mould our day varies from person to person. All I can do here is encourage you not to compare, and instead concentrate on what you do have power over. You can spend your energy thinking about Sally round the corner who should never complain about work because she's self-employed and can make her job what she wants, while you're in a big corporation operating under very strict rules or in a zero-hours contract at the whim of your employer – or you can focus on making your situation more enjoyable. Forget me, forget Sally, and concentrate on yourself and *your* process. Of course, it can be really shit to look around and feel unhappy in your position while others are having a blast, and you have every right to complain about or envy that, but you also have a duty to yourself to focus on what you *can* change and make the most of. The grass is greener where you water it. Just concentrate on yourself, for yourself.

Now that's out of the way, let's think of this chapter as the practical implementation of the first chapter, where we talked about micro-passions and self-actualising. For me, the two main elements that comprise a happy and fulfilling working day – no matter which tasks that day entails – are the ability to get into my flow and being free to practise creative thinking. Sounding niche and not-so-life-changing? Read on ...

We talked about flow a little before, but we're about to talk about it a whole lot more. (Feel free to rap that rhyme if it makes you more excited about the concept. You're welcome.)

The concept of flow was developed by happiness psychologist Mihaly Csikszentmihalyi in his fascinating book, *Flow: The Psychology of Optimal Experience*. Born in 1934 as a Hungarian in Italy, Csikszentmihalyi was a prisoner of war as a child and went on to write a seminal work about finding happiness within work and how important it is in our lives. Csikszentmihalyi reinforces the idea that no matter who you are or where you come from, you need to put effort in to be happy in your work. He points out that this work wasn't exactly a discovery, and that 'people have been aware of it since the dawn of time', but he did carry out important research on its direct relevance to our feelings around work, and creative work in particular. We often think that happiness at work is low on the priority list, but why should it be when we spend so much of our lives working? Whatever it is you do, you deserve to find joy in your productivity and in the tasks that you are good at.

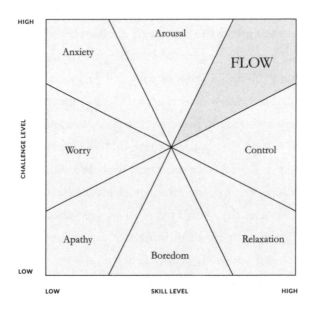

High skill level + high challenge level = flow

I love this concept. To lean on its official definition, flow occurs when you undertake a task in which your skill level and the challenge you're faced with are equal. It could be anything, from solving a complex maths problem where you know you *could* get to the solution, to conceptualising a campaign when that's your *thing*, to getting lost in a painting or cooking up a storm. Crucially, Csikszentmihalyi identified through his research that people were at their most creative, productive and happy in a state of flow.

This may sound quite a lot like deep work – and haven't we already talked about this? Yes, and no. The way I see it, flow sits *within* deep work: a state that you reach when you apply the concentration of deep work to a task that is the perfect balance of high skill and high challenge. In other words, any time you're flowing, you're also deep working – but not all deep work will lead you to flow.

You could see it a little like this:

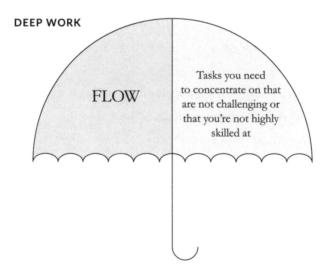

DEEP WORK

FLOW

Tasks you need to concentrate on that are not challenging or that you're not highly skilled at

Or, more like a normal person (boring), like this:

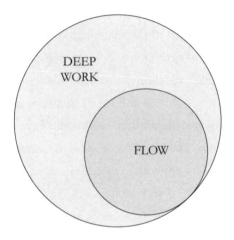

In my opinion, getting into your flow is the best kind of deep work, and is essential to enjoying your work rather than just enjoying its results. While there's a lot to be said for *all* deep work helping you feel fulfilled and happier as a result of your output, tasks in which we can flow will inevitably be more enjoyable. Call me the ultimate nerd, but have you ever had that feeling of happily plodding through a task, feeling the challenge but confident you are capable? That dizzying feeling where you lose all track of time, absorbed in what you're doing? *That* is happiness in work. *That* is enjoying the process rather than just the product. And we all deserve more of it. It may seem trivial, given that happiness from an hour or two is not exactly sustained happiness – but is constant happiness in work even a thing, or a pipe dream we're convinced that everyone else has and we need? Surely – as we discussed in Chapter 1 – we should be working to litter happiness throughout our working days, and if we had at least one flow state per day, we'd be well on our way to doing that.

My explanation of the flow concept so far may not sound that life-changing, but my excitement for flow gives my enthusiasm for time-blocking a run for its money, so brace yourself. Let's get into the theory first, then we can talk about how you can implement flow practically to improve your daily work life.

According to Csikszentmihalyi, there are ten factors that accompany the experience of flow (but note that you don't need all ten, all the time, to be flowing):

1. Clear, attainable but not too 'easy' goals
2. Strong concentration and focused attention
3. The activity is intrinsically rewarding
4. Feelings of serenity; a loss of feelings of self-consciousness
5. Timelessness; a distorted sense of time; feeling so focused on the present that you lose track of time
6. Immediate feedback
7. Knowing that a task is doable; a balance between skill level and the challenge presented
8. Feelings of personal control over the situation and the outcome
9. Lack of awareness of physical needs
10. Complete focus on the activity itself

I find it very interesting that Csikszentmihalyi researched and wrote his book in the twentieth century – a period of rapid technological change – and identified that what we needed was essentially a state of mindfulness in our approach to work, despite not having seen how mobile phones would break up our days with constant distractions. In this regard, his theory of flow and its importance to fulfilment in work feels even more pertinent today than it did when he first introduced it. With that in mind, I'd like to add a modern-day factor to the list above. It's implied in the 'complete focus', but I think it's important to draw out given the working world of today.

11. If you're in a state of flow in 2021, you probably haven't checked your phone in a while. It seems necessary to state that this is now a symptom of flow – the world of notifications floats away, and while I'm in flow I don't want a notification, phone or email to be anywhere near me. Unheard of for a Gen Z, eh?

Csikszentmihalyi also suggests that a state of flow is easier to achieve when:

- You have a specific goal and plan of action
- It is an activity that you enjoy or are passionate about
- There is an element of challenge
- You are able to stretch your current skill level

In this sense, he argues that flow can encourage us to learn new skills and increase the challenge of what we're doing: 'If challenges are too low, one gets back to flow by increasing them. If challenges are too great, one can return to the flow state by learning new skills.' What this means for us is that flow is not only useful in the moment, but it also pushes us – even subconsciously – to become more skilled at what we're doing and to seek out new challenges in order to flow more. In other words, you're going above and beyond in your work, while also enjoying more flow in your day – double whammy!

This might be starting to feel like a lot of work, for more work, but I need you to stick with me here. Sure, you can do everything to the bare minimum and you'll get them done, no one's telling you otherwise. But if you want to enjoy your work *and* create good work, in shorter amounts of time, it's time to get flowing. Flow isn't a chore, it's a gift – and one we can give ourselves more of.

If you're ready to welcome flow into your life, the first step is identifying which tasks get you flowing. We can reach a state of flow in a far greater number of ways than we might initially think, and in reality, you probably flow a lot more than you think you do (and not just monthly, amiright ladies). It might not seem like a difficult or challenging thing to create a mind-map – after all, some might see it as just scribbling down some thoughts and letting your mind run with it – but boy, there's nothing that gets me into a flow like conceptualising. What's important is not whether a task 'qualifies' in your mind for this equation of a high-skill, high-challenge state of flow, but that you learn how to acknowledge when you're in your flow and understand what it is that got you there, and then implement this throughout your working days. Think about how some tasks might make you *feel*: losing track of time, giving full concentration, fulfilment, a sense of 'I've got this', but not to the point of boredom or complacency. Any task that makes you feel 'in the zone' like that can be your flow.

The FlowFlight

Ideally, getting into our flow is just about getting settled and getting going, but we all know that can be hard to do, even when we love and are highly skilled at the task ahead. Instead, it's important that we understand *how* to flow so we can increase the amount of flow in our day-to-day lives; we need working rituals to make it fully optimal, similar to deep work triggers. The difference is that, because the task at hand is something we're already interested and skilled in, we'll likely find the flow headspace easier to get into. For me, there are three clear stages of flow, and I think the best way to explain the process is to think of it as a plane journey (yes, you read that correctly).

FLOW ZONE / IN THE ZONE TIME

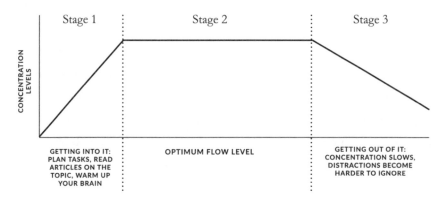

STAGE 1

The plane is on the runway. The engines are running, there's a clear destination in mind, we just need to get up to speed and build up momentum to take off. I usually give myself ten to twenty minutes to 'take off'.

Defined by: You could be any amount ready to go, but you don't feel 'in' it yet. You might need to transition from a very different task, or be over-excited from just having had an energetic conversation and finding it hard to settle down and concentrate. You're susceptible to distractions, and have to force yourself to *commit* to beginning the flow in order to take off. Sometimes, when I know I'm about to start a flow task, I'll be raring to go – I just read one article and I'm off. But because the majority of my working days contain many different types of task, I'll often feel particularly distant from what I'm about to start (especially later in the day), no matter how much I love doing it.

The important thing is to remember that even flow tasks you love will sometimes feel like a chore to begin with, and to be patient with yourself while you're still in this taking-off stage. Sometimes, the last thing you'll want to do is get lost in a task when you've been up to your ears in stress all day. Even though you know it will get you into that happy and productive flow state, you'd rather just push through surface-level work that uses minimal brain power. I know I'm my own worst enemy when it comes to allowing myself to do things I enjoy amid stress; I often feel as if I should be tackling the noise first rather than working deeply on a task I enjoy. Really, this is just me getting bogged down in short-term gratification and the validation of combatting small, stress-relieving tasks rather than spending an hour flowing in something I love. Learn those downfalls, especially when self-sabotage creeps in, so that you can combat them effectively!

STAGE 2

We're in the air! It's smooth sailing, autopilot now. You're enjoying the in-flight entertainment, maybe even sipping a complimentary bubbly and eyeing up those salted peanuts you never asked for. It's all systems go: you're steadily and systematically flowing through your task, enjoying being up in the clouds.

Defined by: You are IN, baby, fully absorbed in the task, working through it systematically and feeling confident in your destination. I LOVE this feeling. You know it might be a challenge to get there, but you are uninterested in the outside world and if anyone tries to interrupt you, you'll almost definitely hold your hand up like your mum used to do when you'd interrupt her on the phone.

STAGE 3

Cabin crew, please take your seats for landing. This part takes a few different guises. Ideally, it's a nice, planned landing into destination end-of-flow, but sometimes you have to descend, stop off at an airport along the way to refuel and recoup. It won't be productive to power through, because ya just ain't got enough fuel. Accept the descent, land safely, then take off again to the same destination when you're ready, or move onto your next task. Alternatively, sometimes I crash-land pretty suddenly and it takes me a little longer to go again – it might even be the end of flow for the day. It will all be dependent on you, the task and the day.

Defined by: Your concentration is beginning to lapse and distractions are becoming harder to ignore. You might be itching to check your phone or emails. I know this happens gradually with my FlowFlights – I don't even realise it's happening, and suddenly I'm on some faraway website in the name of 'research', or have autopiloted back to my phone. This is normal; no matter how much you love something, you have your human limits.

Your flow stages might be different from mine. The key is to identify them and be able to make them happen. You can't expect to use your flow to your advantage without first understanding it and knowing how long you can be 'in the air' before you need a refuel, or how long it takes you to take off. Listen to yourself, learn, then implement. For example, it takes me ten to twenty minutes to 'take off' on a normal day, but it's far more when I'm tired, or if I've just finished a very different task right beforehand. Take note of these repeated traits you have and use them to learn about yourself and your flow habits.

How to identify your flow triggers

Your flow triggers are what you'll need to get into the air and on that FlowFlight to destination productivity and fulfilment. In our high-paced, distraction-filled lives, there's rarely a chance to jump right up to 30,000 feet and into our full flow. While you're likely to be able to get into your flow a little quicker than other deep work sessions, you'll still need to identify what gets you into the zone, and set aside an amount of time within your time-block to it. Any deep work triggers might work here (see page 58), but I find that my favourite flow triggers are ones that are related to the task:

- Reading a related article
- Watching a YouTube video on the topic
- Listening to a related podcast
- Reading some of my previous work on the topic

Ideally, your triggers will have you itching to start the task, but you might become so engrossed in the trigger – for example, reading an article or chapter on the topic – that you find it hard to break yourself away. Set your parameters prior to starting and commit to them, and remember that sometimes you just need to start and throw yourself into it.

How to look after yourself during flow

Time for a small PSA. While it's evident that flow is incredibly beneficial and fulfilling, it also has its downfalls. As with anything that 'makes us forget about our physical needs' and demands 'complete focus', flow can make us throw our healthy working practices out the window. (You know when you've needed a pee for hours but can't make it up from your desk?) It's so important to be able to flow while also taking time for breaks; rest assured that if you don't manage your flow properly, you'll be susceptible to short-term burnout as early as 11am, and that certainly won't help your productivity or the enjoyment of your work. I could share far too many instances of when I've started an early flow session with the best of intentions and got so deep into the task that I don't want to stop (Stage 3 never initiated – Houston, we have a problem). I think I'm doing the right thing, pushing through just to smash it all out, but once done my brain is *fried* for the day, and the fulfilment quickly wears off when I can't concentrate in any of my meetings or tick off any essential TDT items.

To give you an example, just last week I was designing a new collection I cannot wait for. (For context, I don't design all our collections at TALA – I'm not a designer, but I do love fashion and I selectively design ones I'm particularly inspired by.) The design process takes a number of different stages – from trend research and inspiration I've gathered over the last few months, to talking to the team about the concept and our capabilities, brainstorming the campaign, to drawing up the individual pieces. It can take anywhere from an hour (if I'm doing only a few parts of the process), to an entire working day (when I'm taking full control and shooting for the stars with an entire campaign plan).

On this particular day, I started off by looking at trend research in order to put together a brief for the design team. I was meant to be working on this from 9 to 11am, then on calls until 2pm, then back to another project/deep work time-block. But my initial work on the collection led me to such specific ideas for the marketing campaign that I started to conceptualise that too, and before long I knew the exact pieces I wanted each model to wear. (And by 'before long', I mean two hours in.) I was on such a roll that I just powered through my time-block, postponing my calls, pushing everything out of the way – because, hey, this is important! However, by 3pm I was done in, maxed out on inspiration and planning.

Despite it being relatively early in the work day, my brain had officially overworked its engines. All I could do was lie on the sofa, wide-eyed, feeling equal parts accomplished and drained, but in reality having only done one of the few tasks I needed to get through that day. What I should've done was stop at a reasonable, pre-arranged point – or perhaps with a little overflow – and hopped on to my scheduled calls, so I could get back into my flow after 2pm. The quality of my work after a break would have been worlds better than it was three or four hours in. My sense that powering through was the good, hard-working thing to do was definitely misplaced, and I certainly would've felt a greater accomplishment at the end of the day if I'd stuck to my well-planned schedule.

Instead, I ended the day with a severe case of flow-itis (don't worry, it's not contagious).

Cause: Overflow – working beyond concentration limits in a sort of trance until you physically cannot work any more.

Symptoms:

- Getting the shakes and headaches because you've forgotten to eat or drink
- Being unable to think or do anything other than lie horizontal, staring at the ceiling and wondering where you went wrong
- Lack of concentration for the remainder of the day
- Inability to come back to the task you were flowing on, due to feeling like you've fully maxed out and never, ever, *ever* want to see it again

Of course, the above symptoms can be true for deep work, too, but that's more likely to be that you've just pushed yourself too hard, rather than being so engrossed in a task that you can't stop. You're far more susceptible to falling into this trap when in a flow state, because deep work that isn't flow is just concentration and discipline. It's far more tempting to continue a task even after you'd told yourself you'd stop if it's a task you're actively enjoying. Trust me, this predicament is *very* easy to fall into, and easier still if you rarely enjoy the rest of your work. You'll find that you get a sense of misplaced accomplishment as you burst through that two-hour time-block, triumphant that you're so absorbed in your task that you can keep going forever. But don't be tempted to reach breaking point: you need to maintain healthy working practices in order to make flow useful for more than just the time you're in it. Think about it: if it takes you around fifteen minutes to get into it and you can successfully flow for 1–1.5 hours, there is little to be gained (and a lot to be lost) in extending your flow, rather than just concluding your session, taking a break and revisiting. You're going to have to land sometime, so it might as well be with your engines in good enough condition to take off again. You could have the best flow session in the world, but if you can't work after it or you never want to see that important task again, that's a very short proportion of successful flow. By ignoring healthy working practices to blitz a task beyond your limits, you'll ruin the benefits flow can bring in favour of short-term gain and instant gratification.

I guess what I'm trying to say is that there is a middle ground between ace-ing your flow, and overflowing into flow-itis. Healthy working practices are the key to helping you find it, and thankfully, there are lots of preventative measures you can take to avoid the dreaded flow-itis.

1. **Define your flow.**

    a) **Time:** How much time are you intending to spend on this flow? For me, I know it shouldn't be more than two hours. Any more than this and, while I might feel the self-gratification of those hours worked, I will end up less productive beyond this point. I often even start my session slower than I should, knowing I'll be going for a while. Tasks are liquid – they'll fill the time you give them – so keep it short and sweet. Of course, this is going to depend completely on you and the task at hand. I've found that these time limits can be bent when I'm writing rather than working on something business-related, for instance, for no discernible reason. The key is knowing your individual limits for each individual task. Practical tips to enforce this include:

    - Setting a de-flow alarm for when it's time to wrap up
    - Planning your flow time for when you have a commitment right afterwards (allow a thirty-minute buffer to shake it off and come back down to earth, or to let your flow spill over a little, only where absolutely necessary)
    - Asking a colleague or friend to come over and break you out of your zone after a certain time

    b) **Tasks:** Which tasks do you intend to do during this time, and what smaller tasks are they made up of? Try to avoid the temptation of adding more when you're already in the zone because you're 'on a roll'.

2.   **Prepare for your physical needs.** You're never going to be stronger than your physical needs, so don't try to fight 'em! Before getting into your flow, make sure you have at least a litre of water on your desk (with a reusable straw if you struggle to drink it, as it will help it go down easier), and keep yourself hydrated throughout your session. Make sure you've eaten before getting into it, but try to avoid foods that cloud your concentration. (Onions, I'm looking at you.)

3.   **Get comfortable.** Set yourself up in a nice workspace, where you aren't hunched over or on edge. You should have full concentration on your flow, not your impending posture malfunctions.

4.   **Separate your spaces.** Keep your flow space for your flow. Start to associate different areas with different things so you allow yourself that autopilot when you get there, even if it's just the difference between the kitchen table and the sofa, or rearranging your bedroom space slightly in the morning before commencing your work. Now, I'm not suggesting you suddenly evict your family to allow a bedroom for admin and another for flow – just make sure you physically separate work and chill.

5.   **I like to move it, move it.** On that note, once you're done, or while you're taking a break, move elsewhere! Go to the bathroom, sit in the kitchen, or just take yourself anywhere other than your flow space. Staying in the same area and just picking up your phone, even in the name of a break, is going to lead you down the temporary burnout rabbit hole. You won't be getting actual rest; you'll just be

distracting your brain by endless scrolling or hopping straight on the notifications that have popped up during your session. Do some star jumps or have a little pace around instead.

Worried you won't be able to get back into flow after taking a break? Cut the crap and focus on discipline. You might simply be too used to operating only when it comes naturally to you, but you need to be able to *activate* flow. Try intentionally not finishing a task you're intending to come back to when stopping for a break, end halfway through a sentence Ernest-Hemingway-style, or plan the work for your next flow-block before you finish. It's all about learning your flow-triggers, and getting back to it when you're replenished.

We've spoken about how to identify and optimise flow, but the question that remains is, how can we add *more* flow into our lives, to make sure we're increasing the enjoyment we get from our work? Put simply, we can either grow the number of tasks we flow in – by increasing our skill level or the challenge faced – or we can learn to recognise the things that already have the potential to get us into flow, and give them more space and importance in our day when planning our productivity method. One of my favourite ways of adding challenge to the tasks I'm doing (which, understandably, doesn't sound that much fun, but increased flow = an increase of all things good) is through going the extra mile in a direction I love (we'll go into this more when we talk about creativity on page 96).

For now, ask yourself this: are you giving yourself enough time to flow? If not, is it because you've been programmed to believe it's over-indulgent to spend time on a task you enjoy rather than whizzing through it, even if it means doing it better? Is it because your job doesn't allow for it? If so, could you add more micro-passions into your day by taking on more responsibilities in areas you love? As an added bonus, that's one of the most effective ways of shaping your career in the way you want, as it'll help you move on to roles that have more of those elements you love. Let me be clear: flow is just one way to add enjoyment and fulfilment to your working day. It is not the only way, and it's also not always possible, especially when working on menial tasks that aren't as challenging as we'd like. But if you can harness your flow and engage in it if not daily, then at least weekly, you'll find yourself getting to Friday evening with a greater sense of satisfaction.

Creative Uniqueness

When I worked at IBM, my role was *very* admin heavy. We're talking, *we-work-in-a-tech-company-why-isn't-this-being-done-by-a-machine*-type work. My highlights within the job would be anything that was done differently: revamping my boss's bulletin to the team, or turning our company analysis into *much* nicer, clearer documents. I started to realise that no matter what I was doing, the more creativity I brought into my job, the more value I added to both my work and the greater the fulfilment I got from doing something that was uniquely *me*.

> **❝ Creative uniqueness**
>
> The idea that our uniqueness is our creative power. Because we are all unique, we can automatically differentiate our approach to a task, resulting in what can only be seen as a sort of creativity as a result of this uniqueness. **❞**

When I'm talking about creativity here, I'm not talking about drawing a picture or making a graphic for your Instagram feed. I'm referring to the creativity we have in approaching any task, due to the sheer fact that we're all unique. Creative uniqueness might be a better way to describe it (because who doesn't love a new buzzword?). The beauty of creative uniqueness is two-fold: it makes you and your work more valuable because it can't be easily or originally replicated by someone else; and that feeling of being valued in your workplace is going to add satisfaction to your life. It's a win-win situation, for you and your employer. Make yourself irreplaceable, then enjoy knowing you're irreplaceable.

The importance of creative uniqueness rises with each passing year. We live in a world of automation, personal brands and saturated markets. Your uniqueness is your power, it's your edge, it's what differentiates you from the increasingly sophisticated and accessible technology popping up left right and centre. I know this sounds like some dystopian exclamation that 'we live in a world of machines', but look at it from a positive and realistic point of view. Machines have got the boring stuff down: automation is *great* in a way because it means that we, as humans, get to use our brains to do what only we can do and harness our own personal power. Innovation is needed more and more at every level – and I don't just mean innovation in the way of coming up with new technologies or starting a new business, but the innovation we can bring to how we approach our day-to-day tasks.

I've always been stumped by our educational system's lack of appreciation for creativity. Funding for the arts always seems to be on the way down, dancers are being told to retrain in cyber security, and while there's some value given to explicitly creative tasks at school, like art and music, the system as a whole doesn't allow you to approach anything else creatively. We're taught to tick boxes and get the marks, to get it *right* rather than to approach it differently and potentially even create a *new* correct answer where possible. There's a lot of merit in getting things right and having the discipline to do what we're asked – we all know that. But the reality for many of us is that as soon as we graduate from education, we're faced with a world that increasingly values creativity highly, even if it doesn't know it.

There are multiple ways of getting things right, and the best ways to do so involve your own unique approach to the task. You owe it to yourself (and the task at hand) to make your work *your* work, not someone else's. Of course, it's up to us to establish the extent to which we can do this in each job and each task, but I truly believe we can certainly do it a hell of a lot more than we thought we could when writing exam answers checked against a mark scheme. I guarantee that the instant you give yourself the freedom to pursue your own thought processes, you will find yourself enjoying the journey a lot more.

As with our other lists of triggers, I find creativity triggers increasingly important for allowing improved creativity across my work. Your creativity triggers may be different to mine – I haven't called it creative uniqueness for nothing – but a few of them are pretty universal. Find yours, use them, then switch them up as and when you need to, acknowledging the fact that your practices will evolve and change. I want to stress that these are still useful even when you don't think you explicitly need to be creative in a traditional sense. The more you use these triggers, the better quality your work will be by allowing your creative uniqueness to seep into even the most uninspiring of tasks. Creativity is your mechanism to innovation, so let's get those cogs turning.

Think of creativity triggers as like drifting off to sleep: you have to untether yourself and let your mind run free. And I know I probably sound like your mother by now, but it's unlikely that any one of these hints will work with your phone buzzing next to you, so put it in another room or at least on 'do not disturb'. If you're going to go after creativity, don't allow yourself to half ass. As the people say, do it with your full ass.

I've split these creativity triggers into instant and lifestyle triggers, ordered by how they can be implemented into your life. Use the instant triggers for when you need creativity here and now, to get you going in your flow or deep work, and consider adding more of the lifestyle triggers to your routines and rituals for longer-lasting creativity.

Instant Creativity Triggers

You won't be able to do all of these, and some will make absolutely no sense to you. Try them out and find what works for you (I might as well copy and paste this phrase into every paragraph at this rate, but that's only because it's true). Mine *totally* depend on my mood or headspace – I usually need quiet when coming from an extroverted activity, and stimulation when coming from desk-work. Try these a few times, scrap them if they don't work, note what does and do more of it!

1.   **Read.** Read a few pages of a book you love. It'll let your ideas brew and stimulate your thoughts.

2.   **Write.** Write a few sentences about absolutely anything. Just get writing and let your brain out on paper. I find writing the weirdest sentences – just starting to write about my day or how I'm feeling – really gets my creativity flowing.

3.   **Make a mind-map.** A personal favourite! Even if it's not a fully developed mind-map of all your ideas, you'll be amazed how much of a difference just playing word association can make with the task you're about to begin.

4.   **Draw.** Draw an unrelated picture and allow your mind to flow. How about a stickman representation of the scene around you?

5. **Listen to a podcast.** Preferably one related in some way to what you're about to do, though unrelated works too. I think it's the conversational style that helps me the most here – almost like having a conversation with a friend. I find ten to fifteen minutes of a podcast untethers me from distractions and notifications and gets me into a conversational headspace, ready for ideas.

6. **Have a conversation.** Tell a friend about the task you're about to do. It might change your perspective or help you develop your argument even further. It might shine a light on new angles you wouldn't have thought of tackling. Having another opinion doesn't hurt and, as they say, you never know something properly until you can teach it.

7. **Anticipate your dream reception.** (Not wedding reception, unless that's what you're planning.) What do you want people to say about your work when it's complete? 'Original', 'innovative', 'a fresh take' – whatever it might be, set intentions for how you want it to be received, and keep that in mind as you try to make it happen. This is what I did every time I was struggling with writing this book, and especially when I was deciding whether to write it at all. Envisioning what I wanted the book to add to people's lives and how I wanted them to talk about it is what allowed me to position everything in my mind and know what I was working towards. I'll let you be the judge of whether it's worked or not!

8. **Change your scenery.** If you have the option, walk to a local café or sit in the park – a change of scenery *always* helps. Sitting at your desk isn't always the most inspiring place to be, especially if you've been there all day.

9. **Watch a TED Talk.** Concentrate and take notes on it – what do you and don't you agree with? Warm up your critical thinking and your creativity will follow.

Lifestyle Creativity Triggers

These are for implementing more widely as part of your general lifestyle. Of course, you won't be able to implement them last minute to get into your flow or deep work, but they're definitely worth bearing in mind to optimise the amount of time, space and capacity you have for creativity in your day.

1. **Quiet.** The most important of all, and manifested in a number of ways. Allow yourself to experience mental quiet, however this comes best to you. It could be through instant triggers like working out, running, meditation, walking, taking a bath, or any number of personal methods. Let your brain escape the busyness of the world around you at least once a day and create space for those new ideas.

2. **Take time off.** Creative ideas won't have space to develop in your brain without time off. Sometimes your brain has to operate on a one-in, one-out policy – just like everyone's favourite bar on a Saturday night – in order to allow space for new ideas to come in. Of course, this isn't always possible in the moment and probably isn't what you want to read when you have a time-pressured task you're hoping to get creative on, but bear this in mind for the future, or take ten minutes if you can.

3. **Have fun.** On the subject of breaks, get out and let your brain play. Let yourself break out of that cyclical thinking rut that you probably don't even know you're in.

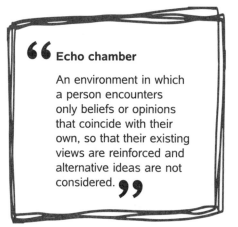

Echo chamber

An environment in which a person encounters only beliefs or opinions that coincide with their own, so that their existing views are reinforced and alternative ideas are not considered.

4. **Talk to different people.** Keep your world diverse, and don't seat yourself in an echo chamber. Agreeing with people is important, and there's nothing better than discussing things you're passionate about with someone who shares those passions, but keep that world varied or risk remaining static in your ideas and beliefs.

5. **Stop chasing perfection.** A blank piece of paper can sometimes scare your creativity away, so just get something down to start, and hold off on casting judgement. It's so easy to put off getting anything on paper until we think it's the right start, the right angle, or until we have the right vision for what we're about to do. Perfection is your enemy here. You need to get going to produce any work, let alone *good* work. The biggest thing I struggled with when writing this book was exactly that: *starting.* As soon as I accepted that the first sentence of each chapter was almost certainly *never* going to make it to the final version, the work started to flow much more easily. Just get started!

6. **Mix it up.** Are your current rituals not working as well as they used to? Give yourself some space from them and allow yourself to change them up. Sometimes even just mixing up your morning routine can help. Try something different, even if only for a day, and you'll be surprised at how far it can go to get you out of a rut.

7. **Sleep more, and better.** Sleep is *so* important for just about everything, but rest assured (pun very much intended), creativity will be the first thing to go when you're not well rested. Read Matthew Walker's *Why We Sleep* if you need to be persuaded.

So, how do you know when to take the time to mind-map, relocate to a café and insert your creative uniqueness, and when to bash it out as quickly as possible because it just needs to be done? And how do you introduce creativity in a workplace that doesn't seem to outwardly welcome it? It's all about *knowing your task* and *knowing your audience*.

If your manager just needs some data, it probably won't be the best use of your (or their) time to put together a full-on PowerPoint *just* to make it unique. You need to be able to judge what's appropriate and what's going to add the most value to your work, and it's certainly not going to add value if you take three times longer because you're making it look pretty. There's nothing more frustrating than needing something quickly and having to wait for someone because they're trying to show off their creativity. In order to establish what the situation is, keep the following questions in the back of your mind:

Knowing your task

- What's the deadline on this task – how much time do you have to think about it differently?
  - If not much, maybe keep an eye out for another opportunity. If you think another way would make it quicker in the long run, but take time initially, perhaps wait and spend time on your new process for the next time it crops up.

- Is it a tick-box task because of necessity and need for speed, or because 'that's just how it's always been done'?
- Do you think this task is already optimised for what it needs to deliver?
- How much value will creativity add vs the time it will take you to add that creative value? If it will only add 0.001 value even if you come up with the best possible solution, is it worth spending time and energy on it?

Knowing your audience is a little more nuanced. You want to please your manager, but you also want to enjoy the process and add your creative uniqueness. This may take a little trial and error to learn where the balance lies, and it'll depend on the person how much they appreciate these changes. However, there are some general questions you can ask yourself in order to help you figure that out:

Knowing your audience
- How do you think your manager will react to things being done differently? If you're not sure, ask yourself the following questions:
  - Do they often do things differently themselves?
  - Do they bounce ideas off you, and do you feel like you could do the same?
  - How have they reacted to changes in the past?
  - Would you describe their management style as 'micro-managing'?
  - When you were asked to do the task or commissioned for the work, did it come with very clear, detailed instructions, or was the brief more open-ended?

o Is the person you're doing the job for an expert in that specific field, or are you the more qualified person?

- Even if your manager doesn't seem like someone who will appreciate things being done differently, that doesn't mean you should never try. Then it's about how you approach it. Some tips for this include:

  o Discuss your approach with them when they give you the brief, rather than once the work is done.

  o Phrase your approach as a suggestion or a question rather than a *fait accompli*.

  o Be strategic about what you put forward. Pick those ideas that you feel most confident in first to build a bank of trust.

All of the above will help you establish the extent to which you can bring your creative uniqueness to each task.

The more you get to know your audience and your task, the more confident you'll become, and the more you'll get it right on a creative level, too. The ability to create and apply this uniqueness is directly linked to how much you believe in yourself and your ideas, and you owe it to yourself to become confident enough to make this approach your norm. But in order to do that, you're going to have to get comfortable with failure. Confidence is key, but *arrogance* is not your friend: you're unlikely to always get it right at first, and that's okay. There will inevitably be things you haven't thought of that mean your idea isn't actually the best one, but failure is *good*. It will – perhaps confusingly – be your biggest confidence booster.

There are a few ways to fail and build your confidence:

1. **Find your champions.** In a hierarchical workplace, you need champions. Who are those people who believe in you and your

efforts? If you don't have one (or more) yet, you need to identify them. These people will not only build your confidence through their confidence in you, but they'll also provide an authoritative voice of support and be able to champion your ideas in rooms where you aren't present.

2. **Have conversations.** Much like finding your champions, you need to suss out the people around you. Talk to your manager or the person you report to about your desire to do something a little differently and see how they take it. You can gauge how and when to implement this according to their reaction. For example, if they seem open to the idea, let them know how you're going to approach the task, and that you will hand it in before the deadline to allow space for error and feedback. They should appreciate that you've been mindful of doing something that might not work, and that you're building in time to correct it. As an employee or contractor, it also takes a little of the pressure off because you know there is time to make changes if your manager doesn't agree it's the right approach at the end. This will give you more free rein, rather than feeling like it *must* be right or you've just screwed up the whole project.

3. **Trial and error.** Try new things, and commit to knowing that they might be wrong. How about handing in two different versions of your task, one being how you usually do it, and another changing it up a bit? Once again, it takes some of the pressure off your new approach, because you've got the tried-and-tested method at the ready.

4. **Listen to criticism.** You might not always agree, but as long as you're doing work *for* someone (which we almost always are, whether that's a manager, client or investor), you need to take this on board.

Discuss it and back yourself by all means, but if the same criticism keeps coming back, ask yourself why. There's a reason the same comments keep popping up, whether you agree with them or not.

5. **Stress test.** This is by far the most important point here, which will not only boost your confidence but also boost your work. You remember we talked about still being able to produce good work while flexing your creativity muscle? That's where stress testing comes in. Before handing anything in, you need to develop your own way of anticipating criticisms for whatever your idea or approach might be. You can't always ask twenty people for feedback before making the move; you'll need to develop your own methods to refine your ideas. You still won't always get it right – we're only human – but you'll at least make sure you have an answer to the obvious problems, and that your idea is fully developed. Try these methods to stress test before you hand in a piece of creative work:

    a) **Force yourself to come up with three criticisms** of your own work – kind of like the W and T of a SWOT analysis – and have an answer for them. If you can't think of an answer, you need to improve your concept, whether this is a new business, or just a new solution for doing a task at work. This will encourage you to see your idea as *in progress,* rather than fully finalised, and open your mind to improvements. We're all guilty of thinking our first iteration of an idea is perfect, but that's rarely the case.

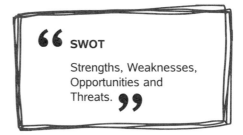

> **SWOT**
>
> Strengths, Weaknesses, Opportunities and Threats.

b) **Read it out loud.** Present to yourself or read your own email out loud. Not in your head: lemme hear ya loud and clear. Do this to a friend or to the mirror, and I guarantee you'll spot mistakes or ways you can tidy things up every single time.

c) **Sleep on it.** Create some distance between yourself and the task if you have the luxury of time – does it still seem like a good idea after twenty-four or forty-eight hours?

6. **Prepare to fail, and see that as a success.** As long as you fail and learn, you're moving in the right direction. The more comfortable you get with this form of failure, the more flair you'll be able to bring.

To be snowflakingly honest, this past year has felt like one long, existential work/life crisis for me. I *know* how lucky I am to do my job. I remind myself every second of every day. I am in a tiny percentage of people who can honestly say they love what they do. But what I realised is that I love my job in principle. I love the *idea* of my job. I run companies that I strongly believe in, that I conceptualised, that I'm able to grow every day with. And yet I also realised that I *hated* my actual day-to-day job. I tried too hard to act like a CEO, and missed the mark on what that meant to me as an individual: why was I there instead of someone else, and how was I the best person for the job? I focused on playing the part rather than playing to my strengths. I was under the (wrong) impression that I had to choose between the two for a number of reasons, including self-doubt and wanting to tick boxes, believing that work should be a chore.

I don't think this issue is discussed enough. Although enjoying your work in any capacity is certainly a privilege, enjoying the product of our work is easy compared to enjoying the process. We spoke about it in Chapter 1, but

I want to reiterate that we have to drop the idea that work always *has to be* a chore. While it is primarily a way to pay our bills, we can significantly reduce the dreaded Monday blues by adding elements we love to our work where possible, and improving the ways we go about them. We need to find a seat somewhere between the utopian idea of fulfilling our purpose and passion each day and loving every second of it, and hating our jobs because we have to do them to survive. While for most it might be harder to find due to the nature of their work, or the number of jobs they have, I strongly believe there *is* a middle ground; we can benefit hugely just from reframing the conversation from unrealistic or defeatist to realistic positivity, and make that reality one we want to be living.

For me, it all changed when I forced myself to discover micro-passions I didn't even know I had, and honed in on my flow. I increased my skills – using anything from courses to autodidacticism – and the challenges I face, by going above and beyond in directions I enjoy. I started reading more, about subjects I loved and was passionate about, rather than solely educating myself on things I felt I *had* to know. I started concentrating on minimising tasks I hate into one time-block, and elevating the tasks that get me into a flow state or that I can add my unique touch to. I've championed my flow to form the main body of my work, and forced myself to time-block and plan accordingly to make this happen. In large part, it's been a process of unlearning the belief that I can't or shouldn't spend time on things I love. I've committed to doing things that in theory I didn't need to do, but I know will challenge me and shape my career in the way I want. And guess what? I can already see the benefits. I enjoy my day-to-day more,

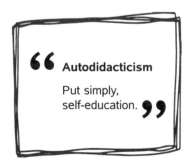

66 Autodidacticism
Put simply,
self-education. **99**

I use my brain more, I value myself and my work more. Of course, I have more freedom to do this than most. And of course, I can't make my *whole* job about micro-passions – I still have responsibilities, things that need to be done; my job is not just a hobby and people's livelihoods depend on it. There will always be loads of shit I hate to do but still have to tackle every day. This chapter is not about 'just do things you love and ignore the rest'. But one thing we *can* do is stop looking for validation and ticked boxes, and instead put energy into making our work work for us.

That's not indulgent – in fact, it's going to be far more productive and effective in the long run. Even if you look at this on a purely productivity-focused level, flow and creative uniqueness are where your work will excel, and they're what's going to help you avoid boreout. We need to shape our day-to-day to suit our micro-passions and our flow, so that we can truly enjoy both our nine to five *and* five to nine. You deserve to be happy (it probably sounds obvious, but it's easy to forget sometimes), and considering the amount of time you spend working, enjoying that work will make a huge difference to your overall happiness. So learn to recognise your flow and its nuances – how to control it, how to increase it, how to enjoy it. Play to your strengths, find what you love and do more of it. The world is finally coming round to the fact that you can build your career on what you love, and work what you love into your career. Take that opportunity where you can.

CHAPTER FOUR

DEFINING SUCCESS

When I was at school, I didn't have a concrete view of what I wanted to be when I grew up. There certainly wasn't one clear goal. Ten-year-old, fourteen-year-old and eighteen-year-old Grace just knew she wanted to be successful. Bold!

I imagine many people would say the same about their aspirations – no child pops out the womb with a clear view of what success looks like. Our general ideas develop as we grow up and start dreaming of what we'll achieve in our hopefully long lives, untainted and unconstrained by reality. Slowly but surely, our perception of success starts to take some kind of shape. I think at one point I wanted to be a lawyer, then prime minister, then 'CEO of a big corporation'. As you can see, young Grace kept her goals very chilled and low-key. One of my favourite family tales stars my sister, Flora, who famously stood in front of her entire primary school assembly and exclaimed confidently 'I want to be a bride!' when asked what she'd like to be when she grew up. I've assured her that I'll caveat this story with the assertion that her everyday feminism has since improved.

You might relate to looking back on your childhood future-job description and rolling your eyes at how adorably out of touch with reality it was. But there also comes a point when our view of success strangely becomes more distant as we get older. We stop trying to figure out what success is for us, personally, perhaps because we start on a 'career ladder' with clearly defined standards of what success looks like in that specific field: showing a collection at Paris Fashion Week, becoming editor-in-chief of a national newspaper, or opening a chain of beauty salons. We see an amorphous bubble of success, more or less completely external to us, which we may or may not achieve in five, fifteen or twenty-five years.

Of course, 'success' has always been a tricky concept to deal with – an issue exacerbated by industrialisation, capitalism and the mythical American Dream. In centuries past, success was more of a clearly defined concept. For some reason, I instantly imagine the 1950s, where, allowing for some significant stereotyping, middle-class women were successful if they married 'well' and had 'happy' children and a clean house; and men were successful if they climbed the career ladder and never saw said children. But as we've thankfully embarked on significant social transformation, and more options have rightfully opened up, those markers of success have become woollier and harder to define. Now, I'm by no means saying we should limit our aspirations or go back to the blatant misogyny, racism and classism of the 1950s – not that we have moved past it either, mind you – and this new level of agency is a privilege that many do not yet benefit from. But it is worth considering that the modern landscape has created a sort of crisis of choice, which has led us to search, often without us realising, for entirely different parameters of what success looks like today.

And we don't have to look far to find them. We're bombarded left, right and centre with the success of others, and it's become second nature to start agonising over what we haven't yet done, where we 'should' be, what we could have achieved. The seemingly democratic nature of our social media newsfeeds has morphed celebrity culture, often without us realising. We could see celebrities in magazines before, so how is seeing them on our phone screen any different? Well, with Beyoncé now framed in the same square box as your mate from school, you can seamlessly flick from your friend's engagement photo to Kim Kardashian's Halloween-decor triumphs, and know that in that time Jeff Bezos has made another billion. We're no longer admiring a mythical child actor in a far-away city who has achieved stardom and bought a house all by the age of three. Instead, we're turning on our phones and following the lives of people seemingly just like us, who are projecting a highlight reel that it is impossible not to compare ourselves to. It's no surprise, then, that we end up subconsciously measuring our achievements against theirs and inevitably find ourselves falling short. This invisible coating of 'relatability' has set external markers of success to a place that's almost impossible to replicate. It has artificially closed the distance between us and the celebrities we follow, leaving us with a perspective that blocks out the vast differences in our lives and circumstances. We don't see the teams, privileges, hours, luck and everything in between that goes into each 'announcement'. And so our idea of what constitutes success has been warped beyond recognition, like an elastic stretched so far beyond its limit that it won't shape back to where it should be. We know what success looks like on our newsfeed, but we have no idea, beyond numbers and impressions and likes and shares and accolades in our bio, what significance it holds in our own lives.

I'm aware I contribute to the very problem I talk about, probably more than I'd like to admit. I'm ten times more likely to share something online when it's good news, and I don't always have the strength to balance that out by posting the lows too. I imagine others in my position feel the same way, and that a lot of us could do more to improve the situation. Having said that, flaws and imperfections have certainly started to be shared more, but this has in itself partly become the currency of much sought-after relatability. While this vulnerability is sometimes shared genuinely, it can also be appropriated in exchange for exclamations of strength and solidarity that come coupled with the fruits of online success: likes, follows and the praise that your 'relatability' makes your highlight reel different from the rest. I worry that we've created a double-bluff of sorts, in which vulnerability has become something that people create and share even when it doesn't really exist, because of the moral kudos and commercial benefits it brings. What this means is that, if the reality of celebrity was disguised beneath a veil of 'relatability' before, with the proliferation of shared vulnerability, it's now become fully camouflaged and nearly impossible to see. But perhaps I'm too much of a sceptic. While I know the online benefits of sharing my vulnerability, it still requires a huge amount of energy that the majority of the time I just don't have. It takes a lot to open yourself up and share your lows to thousands of people you don't know – and hundreds of people you do. In that regard, if genuine, those exclamations of strength are very well deserved.

In reality, a huge Tetris board of opportunity, privilege, hard work and good timing come into 'success'. It's intricate, built up from a series of sliding doors heavily influenced by what we were handed in life. As Malcolm Gladwell wrote in *Outliers: The Story of Success*, 'who we are cannot be separated by where we're from'. So, let's talk about me (that's what us Gen Z love to do, eh?), because I don't believe I can guide you to understanding what success means to you, without opening up about myself. I went to private school; I attended Oxford University; I am white; I am from a family that never pushed me into a certain lane; I grew up in London, the capital city of a developed country, free from war or natural disasters, where I can go to sleep at night almost certain of the fact that I will wake up in a home that's still intact. In a few words, I've been extremely privileged. I've worked since I moved to London at thirteen, but I didn't work because I *had* to, I worked because I was jealous of my fellow private school friends with their pocket money and shopping money when all I got was a *very lucky, no work needed* £25 per month from my parents. (I'll admit, I thought I was genuinely hard done by, which, looking back now, makes me shudder.) I've been privately educated – funded largely through scholarships, yes, but only after years of music tuition. I've come to terms with the fact that no one with a background like mine can truly be 'self-made' when society is this rigged. Being born and growing up in privilege allowed me to explore more entrepreneurial avenues that others may not have ever considered. I was in a position where I could take the time at university to pursue a potentially risky decision like setting up a business, and not everybody can say the same. It doesn't matter that none of my parents' money went into my businesses, or that they didn't really get that I even had a business until a year and a half ago: there are levels to this.

I say all of this so that when you see my Instagram, or read my bio in the sleeve of this book, you can step away from the instinct to compare, and understand the realities that have led to each announcement and achievement. I prefer to lay it all on the table rather than paint yet another picture of what success should look like at twenty-three without providing the necessary context. Following people who inspire you can be fantastic, but you have to consume responsibly and set your boundaries. So, before you judge your achievements against my 'success', ask yourself, did you get the same opportunities? It wasn't handed to me, but I would've had to work a hell of a lot harder if I wasn't privately educated, middle class, white, able-bodied, slim, born in a body I know I belong in, or from a country at peace. This isn't to give anyone a free pass, or to dissuade you from trying because we live in an unequal society, but to put *my story* in perspective. And ultimately your story is about you, not the people you follow or your colleagues or old classmates. Until you define what success is for *you,* you'll be fighting a losing battle. Not because you can never get to where they are, but because you cannot expect to live in parallel to someone else. It's like comparing your Chapter 3 to their Chapter 20, or your novel to their book on knitting for cats.

The more I think about it, the more I believe we need to start consciously seeing success as a relative concept. This is hardly a ground-breaking discovery, but what I've personally come to accept is the reality that I'm never going to feel successful unless I define what success is for me, and if I never *feel* successful, I'll never *be* successful. I don't want to diminish the role that our environment plays in the discussion: where we come from will either limit or broaden what we believe is possible for us, and will help or hinder us in achieving it. My ever-flitting childhood dreams of becoming a CEO or high-powered lawyer were very much a reflection of my privilege; while these roles may not have traditionally been occupied by women, I could certainly see people who looked like me and came from similar backgrounds 'up there'. What we cannot do is say that success is relative, and then condemn people to stay within 'realistic' boundaries – to do that would be a huge injustice to those from disadvantaged backgrounds. You can have big goals and defy all expectations, but that is only valuable if those goals are your own, independent of those people you follow. Get inspired, motivate yourself, look at other people's paths, then create your own.

I want you to be honest. What do you have? What do you not have? Is that going to impact you? Probably. Is that going to stop you? Absolutely the fuck not.

Everyone can have success, achieve success, celebrate success – it's all dependent on what you want and what success *means to you*. This doesn't mean that our personal success can't align with 'traditional' notions of success, but our growing obsession with external validation has meant that we've forgotten that any other possibilities exist. We don't just place too much value on the announcements of others, but also on the announceability of what *we* do. Alongside elevating our natural instinct to compare ourselves to others into a fully fledged obsession, social media has changed the way we process our feelings of success. Here and now, as part of a generation that has only known success as synonymous with outward validation, it took a hell of a lot of soul-searching and discomfort to realise that I'd been getting it all wrong.

I don't think I've ever known what success feels like if it doesn't come with an announcement. When I was as young as fifteen, I remember putting my new sixth-form name in my BBM status to officially declare my excitement over being offered a place at the school. Getting accepted meant less to me than *showing* people I was clever enough to get in. After all, if a tree falls in a forest and you haven't told your friends, your friends' friends, their cousins, and their cousin's aunt's stepmother's godson, did it really happen? Our appetite for sharing success on social media is the equivalent to sending out a round robin of annual achievements. Every. Single. Day. This is fine, at surface value – there's nothing wrong with wanting to post about your promotion or latest press coverage, I'll be the first to say that. If we go back to Maslow's 'Hierarchy of Needs', being loved and 'belonging' is one of our psychological needs, just above basic survival, so it's only natural and human to crave this sense of approval. And social media has opened up access to a whole new pool of love and belonging. But it seems to have reached a point where success means nothing to us *without* this validation. Sure, we have little wins and we might tell a friend or a colleague or a family member, but it's never ultimate, shiny, *#success* until it's widely shareable and validatable.

So why is it that even when we do finally receive that validation, we still struggle to feel like we've really succeeded? We can post on social media and tell everyone about our latest achievement, but as soon as we refresh our feed, those hard-won achievements disappear into the ether and we're back to square one. The comments stop coming, someone else makes a flashy announcement and we're moved along the conveyor belt into the background of not just other people's lives, but our own. The validation we get is too temporary to hold any lasting value or satisfaction, and we find ourselves craving another hit. So we push on straight away and go a step further: do more, achieve more, announce more. Sure, that mentality breeds constant hustle, but the ultimate effect is hugely damaging. It's as if we expect our personal success to refresh just as quickly as our newsfeed. The only way we can stop that conveyor belt is to mentally step off it, to leave it running without us and take our success elsewhere. While we can still benefit from an external celebration of success, we need to move the *value* of success inwards. We need to pause and ask ourselves *why* we want success, and I'm sure as hell the answer isn't really and truly 'to be seen as successful'. Until we do that, we'll never be able to get off the endless treadmill of 'go go go', 'produce produce produce', 'achieve achieve achieve'.

In other words – and perhaps this is the last thing the snowflake-chanters would ever want – we need to stop looking around and concentrate on ourselves. Make our view of success completely and utterly self-centred.

Reject the idea that success is reserved for the few rather than the many. Reject the idea that it has to be big, bold success and can't be the small, accumulative, self-actualising success that comes with enjoying the journey. Reject the notion that you can't celebrate success when you worked for something but didn't achieve that 'end goal'. Success is not all or nothing. You have a choice to make success applicable to you, by defining your own success and letting yourself reach it. You deserve to have success in your life, despite the fact that there's *always* going to be someone out there who's more 'successful' than you.

So, I'll ask again.

What does success mean to you?

What does success look like *for you, personally*?

What would make today successful for you? How about tomorrow? How about next year?

If we're going to start valuing the journey, moving away from one end goal and towards the process, then we have to do the same with our idea of success.

It almost goes without saying that a lot of this stems from childhood, with the emphasis on tests and exams as a measure of academic achievement, and there has been a lot of debate recently on whether this is the most beneficial approach. Obviously, it is important to measure learning progress for various reasons, and we'll talk about the benefits of good goal-setting later on, but when our view of success starts being tied to gold stars and specific accolades at such a young age, it certainly focuses our thinking on the result rather than the process. In other words, it's more about the experience of writing the book than about getting a positive review in the *Guardian*. The way I see it, we need to start thinking of success as continuous, evolving and achievable at every stage for it to align with the view of purpose explored in Chapter 1. We have to allow ourselves the opportunity to be successful in some way at all times, or we're quite literally setting ourselves up for constant failure.

If we want to feel any lasting sense of satisfaction from our achievements, we need to allocate planning, thought and time to defining, reaching and celebrating our successes. If I spent more time writing specific, meaningful goals, I could explicitly celebrate or even just fist pump myself when I reached them; instead, I spend too much energy running around like a headless, insatiable chicken trying to get to the next destination. I don't allow there to be a point of 'success' for me – not now, not ever. I forget about achievements within half a day because I'm constantly going for the next thing and trying to go bigger or do better. And while I'm sure these traits are accountable for my 'success' in part (the above sentence sounds like an advertisement for hustle culture, or an infographic for Shiny Suit Twitter), they are also what makes my success so unenjoyable. I feel ungrateful even writing this, but this chapter is one big @ to me and anyone who feels similarly.

To define our success, we need to first accept that success comes in many forms. There is no one goal, there is no big finish line: there are multiple finish lines, in all different areas of our lives. But in order to enjoy success internally and externally, we need to understand the factors that often influence how we might define success for ourselves. As a society, we haven't fully shaken off historical stereotypes, meaning, for instance, that a woman needs to have a settled personal life with a happy romantic relationship (and preferably a couple of children) in order for her career achievements not to have a big '*but*' right after them. Women are also likely to notice a negative correlation between likeability and professional success – the more successful you are in your chosen career, the less likeable (and more 'cold' and 'bitchy') you are perceived to be. Meanwhile, many men can enjoy success in their work without feeling lacking because they're not in a stable relationship. But as a man, you're likely to be influenced by expectations that you *should* be the breadwinner and financially abundant in order to be successful. I'm not stating these to depress you (and this is by no means an exhaustive list, nor is it applicable to everyone) but we can't identify what success *really* means to you without being, at the very least, aware of the unconscious biases that are at play. At that point, you can combat them or operate alongside them with a critical eye. It's one of the only things that will allow you to confront this world as yourself. Where possible, emancipate yourself from these societal expectations, and create your own.

For me, it all comes down to setting goals – a concrete vision of what my success will look like in ten years, five years, tomorrow and today – and being clear with myself on whether that goal is a stepping stone or something bigger I'm working towards. Different techniques work for everyone, but I believe you need to engage in effective goal-setting, and understand that not all goals are created equal, nor should they be: you need to be able to see the big picture, the middle picture and the small picture. There's a lot of merit in shooting for the stars, but you can't expect to end up there without identifying the steps you need to take to make that dream come true: building the rocket ship, taking off, travelling through the solar system – you get the point. Maybe you can see the big picture – opening up your own shop or getting promoted to head of department, for example – but unless you get some planning in place, chances are you'll have a hard time turning that dream into a reality, or even feeling like you're on your way there. I truly believe that – however eye-roll-inducing you believe 'goal-setting', or 'alignment', or any other journalling buzzword to be – if you spent as much time setting goals as you did wondering when you were going to get there, you'd be a hell of a lot further along.

Goal-setting

I never used to understand the concrete benefit of 'goal-setting' – at most, I'd write a list of goals for the year ahead during the Christmas school holidays with a friend or two. We'd write down targets to the tune of 'get 2 A grades in mock exams', 'make the netball team' and 'stop eating pasta every day' – and then we'd never address them again. (Also, NB, pasta is important and there is nothing wrong with having it every day.) More recently, I've found the practice to be a helpful, if sometimes tedious, exercise in deciphering what *I* want out of my time, and establishing parameters within which I can alter my daily and weekly processes in order to achieve something I wouldn't otherwise have identified. I've forced myself to incorporate goal-setting into my life, perhaps even too frequently, in order to establish better personal boundaries towards success, and address my new cumulative goal of engaging in micro-passions and self-actualising.

In my mind, goal-setting is all about marking a destination with a hefty pinch of planning – it is a science, so let's try to get it right from the off. As with everything we've discussed so far, there'll be aspects of this method that work well for you, and other aspects that won't sit well with you or your lifestyle. Try them all, and mould them to your preferences. As a general rule, the amount of time you spend goal-setting should decrease the smaller the picture gets. For example, you might want to set out half a day for your annual goal-setting exercise, but if you spend more than ten minutes on your daily goals, you'll start to push the limits of what's useful.

WHEN?	
BIGGER PICTURE	Anually
MIDDLE PICTURE	Quarterly
	Monthly
SMALLER PICTURE	Weekly
	Daily

Really? That much goal-setting? Personally – yes, really. It's like steering when you're driving – you can't expect to stay in your lane and en route to your destination if you don't do it.

Annually

This is your big picture moment. Your annual visualisation should be a proper exercise, where you consider how far you've come over the past year, where you want to go this year, and more importantly, where that's going to take you next year and in five years' time. Will it be towards those big-picture goals you have? This is a great time to think about *why* you want what you think you want. I find annual goal-setting hugely comforting and confronting in equal measure – it can be a bit of a shock to analyse where you are today versus a year ago, and it can also help you to realise how much what you want has changed. The incremental, minuscule changes in direction you've experienced throughout the year might not even have been noticeable to you until this point. Our vision of success will be constantly changing and evolving as we grow, which is why an annual, visual check-in with ourselves is so useful. I find it particularly helpful to keep this somewhere visible, like above my desk or on the first page of my notebook; it always seems to catch my eye just when I need it.

In 2017, I remember that my biggest goal was to have a fashion line collaboration with a big brand – think PrettyLittleThing, Boohoo, Topshop. I wrote out my goals for the year, took them to my agent, and explained that this was where I wanted to go and what I wanted to achieve; this is what success would look like for me within the next year or so. A year later, in 2018, I remember sitting down to plan my annual goals again, and realising that this was no longer my main goal – and not only that, but it wasn't even something I'd accept if it were offered to me. I'd realised that I wanted to steer my career away from being an 'influencer' (who wants to travel the world for a living anyway?), and towards being a business owner. I wanted to create a fashion brand of my own, one that prioritised ethical production and sustainability. I realised that my happiness came from a head-down, working lifestyle, and *that* was how I'd self-actualise. That's what success was and is (for now) for me. I had to course correct, and overhaul my goals to take me towards the life I now wanted to build for myself; my definition of success, in the short and long term, had changed.

Annual bigger picture questions

Don't be afraid to dream big, but be honest with yourself about what you *really* want. You deserve that honesty.

1. What is my ultimate career goal?
2. What is my ultimate personal goal?
3. Where do I want to be professionally in five years?
4. Where do I want to be professionally this time next year?

Quarterly

I don't know about you, but ever since school, I still operate somewhat in 'terms' (without the huge summer holiday, much to my dismay). This is also in line with the way businesses operate, which makes quarterly goals a great way to recalibrate and realign with your annual goals. We've talked about your motivation and routines changing with the seasons, so this is also a great way to keep your goals in line with the time of year.

Monthly

We're always shocked at the fact that a new month has arrived, so I would suggest getting that steering in at the beginning of each month to ensure they don't continue to slip by without us propelling ourselves in the right direction. Spend thirty minutes setting your goals, taking into consideration where you are in the quarter and in the year, and then get on with making them happen.

Weekly

This aspect is largely based on the discussions in Chapter 2. Setting weekly goals should fit right into your weekly planning – after all, these should be what you're planning to achieve in the short term.

Daily

Really? Daily goal-setting? Do you want my life taken over by goal-setting, Grace?

I personally find these pretty essential for shaping my day, and therefore my trajectory towards those bigger goals. After all, as the hustlers say, a year

WORKING HARD, HARDLY WORKING

is simply an accumulation of 365 days. You can absolutely get shit done without daily goal-setting, but take it from someone who rejected the idea at first – you should give it a try!

Each day, set yourself three things you *will* get done that day. Just three. Make them realistic, and at the very least tangentially related to your longer term goals. Don't make one of them something you're going to get done in the first five minutes of your day in order to tick something off. You owe yourself more than that. Make each day count, even if it's just about getting shit out of the way to work towards bigger goals tomorrow. How about looking at your daily goals with regards to how you can incorporate the maximum amount of flow and micro-passions into your everyday? It might only be small changes here and there, but I'm sure you'll feel the benefits.

If you're struggling to get any goals down on paper – long or short term – here are some prompts that I find particularly useful. You can use these for all of the different types of goals, just adjust them accordingly.

Goal-setting prompts

First things first, use the words 'I will', rather than 'I want to'. I know it sounds ridiculous, and I feel *very* Gen Z writing this, but I find it really helps me. Plus, no one should be looking in your notebook anyway. This is based on the basic rules of manifestation, but to me, it's more about convincing myself that I can do it. If you cannot write 'I will … ' without feeling fake, you're falling at the first hurdle, and it might be worth asking yourself if your goal is realistic to begin with.

1. A **professional goal** to achieve this year:
    o I will be promoted to manager; I will receive a pay rise

2.   A **professional habit** to instate and do often:
   o I will take two professional development courses pertaining to my industry and/or areas of interest

3.   A **personal goal**:
   o I will to go to therapy once a fortnight

4.   A **personal habit**:
   o I will read ten pages of a book each day

5.   The **feeling** you want to achieve by reaching these goals
   o I will feel more freedom in my daily life and work schedule as a result of these changes

General goal-setting rules

Now that we've identified when to set goals, we need to be clear about *how* we set them. You might be thinking that I'm goal-drunk at this stage, and I wouldn't blame you, but I'd rather be intoxicated by goal-setting than waste time setting ineffective goals.

My favourite goal-setting rules are simple: make sure they're S.M.A.R.T. (as much as I wish I could claim credit for the nifty acronym, this is a well-established tool to help set effective goals):

Specific: clearly defined

Measurable: criteria of the goal is specific enough to *know* when you've reached it

Achievable: attainable and realistic

Relevant: aligned with your overarching views of success and desired trajectory

Time-bound: set the time you want to achieve this goal within – give yourself deadlines

Make sure your goals are all of the above, and you're setting them right.

SELF-CRITICISM	SELF-ACCOUNTABILITY
'I'm stupid, a waste, and I never do anything right'	'What can I learn about myself from what happened?'
'Everything is all of my fault'	'What pattern bought me here?'
'I "fell off" with my routine/ discipline'	'I was human and routine is always available to me'
'Everyone is doing better than me and has it together'	'Humans are messy and I work to consistently forgive myself?'

Let's have a little pep talk. While good goal-setting is incredibly beneficial, we also need to remember that we're human at the end of the day. We can have the best intentions in the world, and we can work really fucking hard, but we can still miss, or shit happens, or we just don't get to where we want to be. The worst part about this isn't the 'failure' itself, it's the effect it can have on our mindset. Keep yourself accountable, but maintain good self-talk. If you allow yourself to fall into a failure spiral, you're more likely to keep falling down. Recognise where you went wrong – were you too ambitious? Did you not stick to your routine? – then set realistic goals which address that problem next time. Don't allow yourself to self-criticise beyond accountability or you'll become apathetic towards your goals and defeatist towards what you can achieve. You can be honest with yourself and hold yourself accountable without hitting your head with a lamp, Dobby-style.

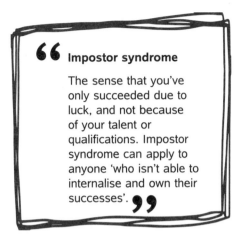

" Impostor syndrome

The sense that you've only succeeded due to luck, and not because of your talent or qualifications. Impostor syndrome can apply to anyone 'who isn't able to internalise and own their successes'. **"**

One of the main areas that can stop you celebrating and therefore experiencing any meaningful success beyond just an accolade is impostor syndrome – the light of my life (sense the sarcasm, please). Impostor syndrome can hold you back infinitely if you allow it to. When you feel undeserving of your success, it's easy to neglect celebrating it, and to hold yourself back from achieving more, to avoid feeling even more of an impostor. I've always been terrified of big-time failure – a company going bankrupt, having to lay people off, letting people down – that is what keeps me up at night, time and time again. But I've also thought, deep down, that perhaps it would bring me a huge sense of relief. There would be nothing to prove any more, no peak to live up to, no trajectory to surpass, no one to prove wrong. How sad is it that, in a world full of so many facets of success, sometimes we'd rather fail just so we no longer have the pressure? It astounds me. Of course, I wouldn't *really* want to lose everything at all, but I do find it strange and irrational that I sometimes fantasise about the release, the freedom, the lack of expectation.

I've since learned that this is another presentation of impostor syndrome, known as the 'upper limit problem'. It's a type of self-sabotage, which manifests as the feeling of 'wanting to fail' or a desire to throw in the towel to obtain relief or freedom. Psychologist Gay Hendricks, who first diagnosed the condition, describes it as a sort of 'inner thermostat setting', which sets an upper limit on how good we'll allow ourselves to feel. When we experience a taste of success we start romanticising the idea of it all going wrong, and become obsessed with the idea that we'll lose our job, that the relationship will end badly, or even – as I remember feeling when I finally approached the end of my university career – that we'll just suddenly drop dead (maybe just me?). This 'thermostat' aims to regulate the feeling of happiness and success back down to a level that we feel more comfortable with by catastrophising what we should be celebrating. Chances are, if you suffer from the upper limit problem, you'll experience this more and more as you approach your predetermined points of success, and it's in your best interests to fight it. Think of it as a sign that you're getting successful, more than you've ever experienced before. The only advice I can offer is to acknowledge it, then ignore it and enjoy your success in abundance.

I still deal with impostor syndrome every day, and it's often only when people criticise me unfairly, discounting my hard work, that I'm able to fight it. I'm able to back myself up and see the hours, the graft, the sacrifice that went into doing something that lots of people were in the same position to do, and didn't. There are always going to be people who are going to talk shit about us – behind our back or to our face. We don't always need to fight them, but the worst thing we can do is join them against ourselves.

I've identified a few ways in which I personally tackle my impostor syndrome. This is undoubtedly something that's incredibly unique to each individual who experiences it, and my methods of coping might do sweet FA for you.

1. Acknowledge that whether you feel deserving or not, you are where you are, and you might as well enjoy it.

2. Some things are easier than they look – that's true for your work, and everyone else's. That doesn't mean you didn't do them, no matter how much or how little work it took.

3. Sometimes you get lucky! So does your neighbour, your colleague, and that person you love to follow for what they've accomplished. Shit happens, but so do good things, and sometimes you're in the right place at the right time, or you meet someone who just so happens to be able to facilitate your next big step. It doesn't discount that you took that opportunity and made it happen.

4. Cutting corners is *smart* as long as you're not hurting anyone. Keep profiting from doing things cleverly, quickly and easily. Cutting corners does not change or diminish your final destination. It doesn't mean you don't deserve to profit from the success you receive – in fact, enjoy it more, because you got there quickly and with less effort. That's amazing!

At the end of the day, we're always going to be able to diminish ours and others' success in the name of luck. In reality, life is a series of good luck and hard work – sometimes you put in the hard work and you still don't get the results; other times you don't put in nearly as much effort and it pulls through. It's swings and roundabouts. Set your direction, drive it forwards, steer, set goals, work hard, then live your life and enjoy your success. Or you can spend your life belittling your own efforts and never celebrating anything you've done. It's your choice.

We've talked about the importance of hard work, how to boost productivity, and how to inject more enjoyment into the work that we do. It's important that we end this section with the reminder that we work hard because there is something we're working hard *for*. And it is our duty to create that feeling of success, in whatever form it might take – whether that's work you consistently self-actualise in, supporting your family, or just making it through another week. Don't let your hard work go to waste by not allowing yourself to define and celebrate your success – we're all guilty of it, but it's not something we can afford to do. We hear incessantly that life is full of ups and downs, but we have the power to create our own fulfilment through holding onto the highs and backing ourselves through the lows.

And always remember that however much you might want to achieve things, if *Working Hard* is starting to make you feel miserable, it might be time to have a little rest. Enter, *Hardly Working*.

hardly working

CHAPTER FIVE

REDEFINING PRODUCTIVITY

My final term at university still stands as the busiest time of my life. An unfortunate, yet entirely self-inflicted, series of complications led to me launching my second business and being examined for 100 per cent of my three-year degree in the space of just over a month. Commendable to an extent, but actually not very clever. I remember it vividly, the dates still etched in my mind from the constant 'countdown' phone apps I'd use to make my impending doom look pretty. Screenshot the countdown, apply it as your phone background and motivation is all yours.

On 29 April 2019, we announced the arrival of TALA, the business of my dreams: a fashion brand that doesn't compromise. TALA's birth, to me, represented no longer having to choose between style, sustainability and price point, and was the culmination of my love for fashion and distaste for the horrors of the fast fashion industry. Bringing the business out into the world was nothing short of thrilling, and was lovingly accompanied by a slew of post-birth Instagram posts, the enthusiasm of which could only be matched by new mothers. On that same day, I was due to hand in 35,000 words of coursework. Then, a week later on 7 May, we were hard-launching TALA into the industry with an amount of stock dwarfed only by the amount we had to prove. That would be after our launch party the night before, of course – the official laws of business dictate that you can't have a launch without a party.

Two days post-launch, on 9 May, I had my main dissertation deadline, which felt like throwing 10,000 carefully chosen words into the void to be judged and criticised (and for me to never read again). Immediately afterwards, I began the three-week sprint to prepare myself for the five three-hour exams that accounted for the final 62.5 per cent of my degree. The beginning of this exam marathon was 27 May, after which hundreds of student-shaped ghosts would emerge from the exam halls with low blood sugar and hand cramps, nervously comparing answers and inflicting a critical inner dialogue with the beauty of hindsight. The remaining four exams were spaced generously over the next ten days, bringing me to the date etched in my brain since I'd received the exam timetable a few months prior: 6 June. It was a date of almost mythical quality, symbolising freedom and success against all odds; the finish line of fighting a three-year battle to run a business at a university that believed in both quality *and* quantity of work – no compromise.

We've all been there, no matter what your 'there' might be – deadlines pelted at us left, right and centre, pulling us in different directions and leaving us feeling drained, overworked and nursing award-winning stress levels.

Much to my surprise, however, everything went to plan, allowing me to fully enjoy the TALA launch. As we sat in the high-rise boardroom of my childhood work-dreams on 7 May, counting down the minutes to 'go time', I'd never felt so terrified and happy in equal measure. I was ready for this company to finally launch after months of pushback and a year of planning, and I was egged on by the eye-watering response we'd had to our announcement. The starting pistol sounded and thousands of people flooded the site. What had once seemed a huge amount of inventory quickly turned into a sea of missed potential as we were out of stock within minutes – admittedly one of the best problems to have.

Moments later, we started to realise that in fact our site was overloaded. The majority of orders might as well have been randomly generated due to what we later discovered to have been a back-end fault on our side. The astronomical revenue numbers on the screen reflected a glitch that allowed us to oversell stock, and orders to process incorrectly. In plain terms, thousands of people were buying pieces that either didn't exist or were misaligned with the inventory, so if you ordered a medium, there was no telling what size you'd actually receive, or whether it even existed at all – like an inconvenient, unsolicited online shopping roulette. I was stressed beyond measure, but admittedly not overly disheartened – these things happen and can be fixed. What I hadn't anticipated was the following two-week-that-felt-like-two-year period in which we had to reach out individually to every single customer, verify their order and often tell them they wouldn't get it, while at the same time popular influencers were receiving and posting about their pre-launch PR stock, rubbing salt in the raw wound of upset customers with unfulfilled orders. Our tiny team, which had little knowledge of what on earth to do, ran through every single option and carried out most of them, all in the hope one would work.

Instead of spending time metabolising meticulously crafted revision cards, I was crying hysterically on the phone outside the library (right beside what I later found out was a single-glazed window – front row seats for the study crew). I was devastated for supportive customers who wouldn't get their orders, and for crying customer service teams (which now amounted to everyone in the company) who'd been working through the night for days. I remember being mortified as silent tears streamed down my face while I desperately posted on my college's Facebook group offering to personally pay any non-exam season students £15ph to add much-needed manpower to our sinking ship.

Back then, I was working to my maximum efficiency and felt like I'd invented diligence; and I was really fucking drained. I hadn't accounted for the emotional tax value-added to my stress, which was already sky-high during the launch of a company I'd poured my heart, soul and reputation into. I hadn't factored in glitch-gate hell breaking loose, and I hadn't acknowledged my need for some sort of weekend or scheduled time off in order to actually concentrate and absorb information come Monday morning's dive back into it all. My human limits had been thrown out the window in exchange for this newfound, finally legitimate, *hustle*.

Strangely, although I was in a constant state of shock, stress and near-hyperventilation, I remember feeling the most validated I have ever felt. I was living the life. I was fighting the good fight. I was hustling the hustle. I was *finally* working as hard as people thought I worked, because I couldn't cut corners to make anything more efficient when they physically couldn't go any faster. I was working until the early hours, and I was putting in *work* like I never had before. No time for rest, no time for anything but work. Don't get me wrong, I'd always worked hard, but this was a whole different ball-game. What was also true was that this way of working was contained within a needs-must amount of time, and my glowing halo of validation and legitimacy would no doubt have come crashing down with concussing reality had I continued this song and dance for any more than a few weeks.

What strikes me as most bizarre about this period of my life is that my sense of being a hard worker only came with an unsustainable – and frankly ludicrous – work rate. It's like rewarding a long-distance runner only if they sprint for the entire marathon, rather than just the home straight: it doesn't make sense, it's not realistic, and if it was even possible it would result in serious injury. In our new attitude to productivity, which is certainly sports-worthy in its competitiveness, there's indubitably a satisfaction that comes with pushing yourself to the absolute limit. By working an eighty-plus-hour week you feel simultaneously punished and proud. In this sense, our lack of concern for our human limits is not just rose-tinted and unrealistic, but an act of self-sacrificial stoicism.

Looking back now, I can't help but ask: why was *this* my vision of optimum 'productivity', when I knew it was unsustainable and also made me miserable? Why was *this* what made me feel validated? Because I could share it? Because I could post an Instagram story at 2am still in the library *working hard*, not just as part of a highlight reel, or better yet a *hustle reel*, but as my full reality? My impostor syndrome was awarded a significant reduction because I could see the time I was putting in, and it looked just like the time that the hustlers I followed on social media seemed to put in 24/7. And while I'm sure that different people experience this pressure to work till the cows come home to varying degrees, it's evidently something a great number of us are feeling increasingly weighed down by.

Let me be clear, now. The reality of my *current* working life goes as follows:

I work very hard, and I am comfortable saying that now (but still, especially so when I'm stuck in a crisis or some other deadline that requires an impressively late laptop-shut). I have days where I'm in my flow and I *don't* take a break, despite that probably being in my best interests. I'm able to produce a truly amazing amount of work when needed, and sometimes crises or deadlines require it. I'm currently spending three days a week writing this book, and still completing my full-time job in the remaining days – but that's a needs-must amount of time with a set goal at the end; it's by no means my everyday reality. It physically couldn't be.

There are days when I work at 50 per cent capacity; days when the most impressive thing I've done is write down my never-realised goals for the day; days when I want to kick myself for not being able to produce anything of note at all. I also now take weekends, *every weekend.* I sleep *at least* seven hours a night (*audible gasps can be heard from the* 'sleep is for the weak' *club*), and if I don't, it's more likely to be because I was out with my friends, up talking to my housemates or watching one-too-many episodes on Netflix, than having some superhuman, supermoral ability to tackle spreadsheets.

During my end-of-university sprint, I neglected to consider the fact that planning is golden, until your brain refuses to go to plan. You cannot rush creativity, prevent hormonal breakdowns or stave off burnout. You can plan how to avoid burnout, but in the spirit of pure output, I didn't. I was convinced that the only thing that would stop me getting everything done was my own laziness and lack of discipline. I've needed time to understand that not working isn't lazy, it's necessary, and we all have to factor it into our schedule.

Calendar entry of 'CHILL TIME' 6–9pm, Tuesday

We are not machines. Our cogs don't always turn in the way we want them to. I am someone who hardly ever says that I can't get something done – not in an 'I can do anything' way, but in the spirit of tough-love, where if I need to do something, I *will* suck it up and do it. It's taken a lot of growing up to realise that I can't ignore the fact that instead of cogs, I have bones and hormones and blood and brains (sometimes). Instead of processing power I have drive and ambition, which ebbs and flows even in the face of routine. And the longer we value ourselves exclusively by output, the longer we miss the point. It's time to stop.

Let's go back to talking about productivity for a second. 'Productivity?' I hear you say: 'I thought this was the *Hardly Working* section?' Or maybe you were ready to skim-read the rest of this book, because how much do you really need to learn about hardly working? How much can you be told about how to spend your free time? Aren't you reading this book to improve your *work* not your *play*?

See, this is where I think we've mostly got it wrong.

I'm definitely not the first to acknowledge that, with the rise of neoliberalism, we've started seeing people as objects of 'human capital'. Our value has become linked to how much we're able to produce, and we're rewarded accordingly within our capitalist structure. Adding to that is the exponential growth in new technologies which has allowed us to multi-task to an unprecedented degree, be it taking a call and writing an email at the same time, watching *Selling Sunset* while responding to an Instagram post, or listening to an educational podcast while making dinner. Technology is productivity's best friend and, when used right, it can help to 'optimise' us. But it's also partly responsible for making us feeling like we're going mad. On the one hand, we don't like to spend waking time not producing in some way; on the other, our brain isn't evolved enough to do two or more things at once at the rate that we're pushing it to. I have grown up with the knowledge I can do 532 things at once – I've never known anything else – resulting in a sort of anxiety around just doing one thing at a time, as if that's lacklustre. I've had to make a conscious personal effort to *stop* doing this and be *present*. Perhaps that's why we've seen such a resurgence in practising mindfulness, and, alternatively, why I've seen older generations often rejecting these 'buzzwords' as, at best, common sense. For them, that was just the standard way of living.

In today's culture, 'productivity' has moved beyond achieving set results in minimal amounts of time, to focusing more on putting in hours, losing sleep and being able to show how *hard* we work. *That* is what productivity means to us – a kind of marketable workaholism. We're then sold this idea of 'working smart' as an alternative, savvy option, but even that doesn't seem to be legitimate unless we also put in a humbly braggable number of hours. In this sense, 'productivity' has lost its value as a desired part of our working lives, and become equivalent to a machine-like churning of output, getting as much work out of ourselves as we physically can before we just pack in one day and, well, die. (Not-so-fun fact: *karoshi* is the haunting Japanese term to describe those who die from a sudden heart attack or stroke caused by excessive overworking, most commonly translated as 'overwork death'.) Or maybe, the churning stops when we realise we can never win this contest, and we take a step back and settle in for the long run. But this only happens after years and years of thinking we're not good enough and we don't work hard enough.

I may be wrong, but I just do not, and cannot, think this is 'productive'.

Thankfully (kind of), there's a lot of research to support this belief. In 2019 (while still part of the EU), the British put in the most hours of work weekly (42 hours a week on average) compared to any other member state, and we're not even the most productive. Meanwhile, our neighbouring European countries are *fantastic* at taking time off. Well below the EU-28 average of 40.2 hours, the average working week in Ireland is 39.4 hours, and it is the most productive of all, with Denmark following closely behind with only 37.7 full-time employee hours per week as their average. Taking a look at our other neighbours, the French (who also rank above us on the productivity scale) have a law that states they legally don't have to look at emails after work hours, nor can anyone ask them to. While negotiating this, unions insisted that new 'disconnect' laws were vital to combat the 'explosion of undeclared labour' facilitated by digital technologies.

Now I'm not suggesting that we need to overhaul our entire working practice legislation yet, but it does go to show that working ourselves tirelessly into the ground is *not* the same as being productive. There seems to be another, seedier and more gruesome possibility taking place behind the scenes, whereby extra hours of unpaid work are allowed to be framed as 'productivity' for the benefit of everyone except the labourer themselves. Alongside late nights at the office with no overtime, unpaid internships and work experience are the norm in many industries. While the UK is by no means the worst when it comes to labour protection, it does become all the more shocking when we learn that other EU countries are proactively fighting this change in work culture by putting further laws in place to protect their citizens as the issue develops. I'm not sure how to 'productively' combat this – after all, we want to be able to work hard and benefit from the fruits of going 'above and beyond', but it certainly casts doubts on the incentive to work hours and hours unpaid in the name of winning a gold productivity star and raises a variety of valid, and very serious, questions..

The idea of a four-day work-week has been toyed with for as long as I've been working (saying that makes me feel mature), and yet it still seems like a faraway, slightly confusing dream. Those in favour argue it to be more humane, and beneficial to output, helping to 'divvy up jobs, encourage local tourism, help with work-life balance and increase productivity', as Jacinda Ardern, New Zealand's prime minister, asserted. The message seems to be that, not only are we pushing ourselves to the brink, but it's also completely and utterly in vain. It's understandable, then, that we're confused by the fact that we're expected to be working through the night, and on weekends, and on Christmas Day, so as to be giving ourselves (or at least, *looking* like we're giving ourselves) the best chance at success. It is so clear to me that there is a sort of golden balance, unique to each of us, in which we actually increase our productivity by taking the rest and recuperation we need. Of course, this doesn't in any way substitute for proper labour laws and better systemic attitudes to productivity, but it's imperative that we start making changes on an individual level, in order to be able to work within our current landscape too.

Yet, while we all *know* that we need to rest and recuperate and live our lives, the main priority seems to be to work hard and make waves. And that's hugely beneficial in a multitude of ways – the fact that the first section of this book is titled *Working Hard* isn't lost on me. But the real tea? *Working Hard* means nothing if you're not engaging in *Hardly Working* as well. I'm not suggesting that we stop working hard and reject the notion of work altogether (I have spent the last four years knee-deep in start-up culture, after all). But our output-obsession has pit *Working Hard* and *Hardly Working* against one another, rather than showing them for what they are: two sides of the same productivity coin. It's about time we redefined our idea of what working hard means, what productivity and hustle entail, to include notions of self-care and rest.

Our current view of productivity is unattainable, unrealistic and, *you got it*, unproductive – and people like me have had a huge part to play in it.

Thankfully, there are many people out there who don't kill themselves at work despite this culture; who are happy keeping a balance of earning just enough, enjoying their job and working at 60 per cent capacity day-to-day so they can finish early and go for a pint or a run or whatever else they enjoy. But what isn't right is that this is seen almost like an act of rebellion within our new working world.

What I find particularly contradictory in the rise of hustle culture is that not all hustle was created equal. There's a discrepancy between the hustle culture I'm discussing – normalised unrelenting busyness and hustle-porn – and those who need to work extra jobs and excessive hours in order to make ends meet. It's one of the fundamental paradoxes of capitalism that work can be both glamorous and ugly; covetable and exploitative. To hustle is to be glamorous, only if it is a choice and confined within certain non-industrial sectors. None of this is breaking news, but I do find it confrontational to acknowledge how we love to shout about how hard we're working if we're in certain spheres, but it stops being 'something to brag about' when that same hard work is no longer a choice. It's glamorous when I post about how many hours I'm putting in because it's underlined by middle-class success. I think part of the glamour comes from the myth that our new working world is modern, slick and, most importantly, far away from the Industrial Revolution and the (still very real) vision of children working for hours in factories.

Of course, our distorted view of productivity is not exclusive to the realms of social media. Hustle culture, in some form, has been a part of office culture since long before *I* existed: which of us can say they never wanted to be seen leaving the office late at night, or never complained to colleagues about extraordinary workloads, or never emailed on weekends to prove they didn't look away from their laptop for a second? It's normal human psychology to want to show off our hard work, and it provides a good way to let off steam and attract the rewards we deserve, too. But I do think there is a multiplier effect of being able to see these signals just about everywhere and on every level (when following your friend one moment, and your favourite entrepreneur the next). It's been taken beyond friendship groups and offices, and become a constant barrage from all directions, inside and outside of work, and no amount of 'no talking about work at dinner' can stop it. Before, when we finally did leave the office, the comparison stopped – now, it continues long after we get home, and the subjects of this comparison are no longer just those in our sight line. Whatever we do, wherever we look, we're subjected to consumption of our friends', friends' friends', idols' and enemies' quasi-performative working habits.

In her essay, 'The I in Internet', Jia Tolentino discusses the rise of the internet and its relationship with how we perceive our own identities. She focuses at one point on the internet's over-valuation of our own voices and political involvement, known as the phenomenon of virtue-signalling. According to Tolentino, the internet is defined by a 'built-in performance incentive', whereby people have begun to assert their political opinions online as a way to signal that they are an innately good person by expressing distaste for 'bad things' and supporting 'good things'. Tolentino asserts that the majority of us do so mainly because it 'intersects with a real desire for political integrity' – we genuinely do want to be good people supporting good things and condemning bad things; it comes from a place of authenticity.

I read the essay nodding along like one of those bobblehead dog toys, and began to think about how this relates to our demonstrations of how hard we're working. In this sense, rather than virtue-signalling, we're intent on *hustle-signalling*. The 'built-in performance incentive' also applies to the hustle-o-meter, which we can use to validate our own productivity via hours spent (and shared) to get there. And much like the authenticity fuelling the signalling that Tolentino describes, we do have a real desire to be a hard-working person who is deserving of success – or at least, not lazier than the person next to us. In a similar way to people posting photos at a protest to show they are good, caring individuals, posting photos of 'the grind' signals to those watching (and ourselves), that we are diligent and hard-working. It seems so *cool* to work all the time, as if it makes us morally superior rather than exhausted and unproductive. You might read that and think it's great – I mean, what's better than an era of inspired, motivated young people, ready to work their butts off to change the world? But, in reality, it's gone too far, and turned into something damaging and *very* confusing.

It has made it impossible to accurately assess what it means to work hard, be productive and, on the other end of the spectrum, what it means to be 'lazy'.

Don't work on weekends? Lazy.

Take a holiday? Lazy.

Don't start work till 9am? Lazy.

Spend your evenings with friends? Lazy.

All work, no sleep, please. Otherwise, are you really made for success? What we're internalising is that you need to make the *ultimate* sacrifice for *ultimate* hard work. It's as though we're living in some sort of *Total Wipeout* course heading towards destination burnout, in which all those stupid (read: very fun-looking) big foam obstacles are actually your body telling you to slow down. It seems a clear sign that our expectations are off if people working regular forty-hour weeks think of themselves as lazy, and I know that I overflow that boundary quite frequently too. If working hard is just a thing we do, how has the 'hard work' standard become unattainable without diving headfirst (or probably more accurately, painfully belly flopping) into a sea of burnout?

The truth is, I don't have any solutions. Realistically, we're not all going to quit social media (though some might argue that is the wisest move), and we're not going to completely overhaul deeply ingrained parts of our workplace culture overnight. I suppose the only piece of advice I can give is, when you consume my content or your friend's content or any other content, remember to take it with both a pinch of salt *and* at face value. A story at 2am in the office means exactly that: someone was in the office at 2am one night. It doesn't mean that they were doing the same yesterday, or that they will do it again tomorrow, or that they were there at 2.01am, or even that they were there earlier in the day (for all we know, they might well be nocturnal). We take one piece of a puzzle and extrapolate to fill in the entire jigsaw by looking through these highlight-reeled glasses. Nobody can advise you on what hard work looks like, because it never looks the same. But the one thing all forms of hard work have in common is that they're not about working all the time.

Much like the effects of social media on our body image, we need to start a conversation about our productivity image. How do we see ourselves in regards to our working habits, and is it accurate? Is it sustainable? Is it just the amount of time we intend to spend working and in fact not lazy at all? Or is it distorted through comparing ourselves with the people we see around us on- and offline, creating a sort of productivity and work-ethic dysmorphia? Would we even *want* to be working as hard or as often as those qualified hustlers? At the very least, having this conversation with ourselves allows us to confront what we *really* want, and where we *really* are versus where we'd like to be.

If we ignore the warping of our productivity image, we risk ending up in a never-ending guilt-pit over the fact that we physically can't work as hard as other people (or, rather, as hard as we perceive them to work), and therefore don't deserve to do as well or enjoy our success. I believe I have this phenomenon to thank for a large part of my impostor syndrome: 'But I don't work as hard as them!' rings through my internal dialogue as I see another '5am club' Instagram story. And if it's had this effect on me – someone generally seen to 'work hard' (thanks, in no small degree, to my hustle-signalling, I'm sure) and who has generated a considerable amount of 'announceable' work – then I'm pretty sure I'm not the only one who feels this way.

When I delved deeper into my own productivity image and *my* hustle-reel, I began to worry that some of this wasn't applicable to the large majority of people. Don't get me wrong, I feel like everyone in our new social-media-driven world is susceptible to this warped view, no matter who they follow or who follows them – it's ingrained in our world more than ever. On top of that, social media bulldozes physical borders, so that if you work within one culture and consume another online, you're likely to feel the effects of both on your expectations. That being said, I'm definitely at the epicentre. I live in a capital city, I consume a worrying amount of media (social and otherwise), I'm an entrepreneur, and the reality of this certainly differs between countries and industries; the examples I've been using are largely extreme representations of the social media, entrepreneur-centric 'hustle' crew who post motivational quotes with lions in the background to somehow symbolise their roaring work ethic.

But the reality is that working parents, non-working mothers, students – just about anyone – is susceptible to experiencing burnout and a warped productivity image. It doesn't have to manifest as working weekends or not taking holiday – in some sectors, it might present as a culture of busyness, or the ability to juggle being a good parent and guardian and smashing that glass ceiling. Whatever your situation, burnout is really fucking hard rather than cool and glamorous – and it'll be significantly more difficult to pick yourself back up after experiencing it.

It's time to take a long, hard look at what being productive actually entails, and to do that, we need to come up with a new definition and celebrate the fact that productivity isn't about working all the time. There needs to be a – wait for it, eye-roll at the ready – *balance*.

I hate what the idea of balance has become as much as the next person. What was a legitimately valuable and beautiful concept has morphed into yet another unrealistic standard of how we should be living our lives. #Balance now represents a morally superior ability to juggle work, social life, working out, relationships, finances, being a good friend, family, and sleep with the skill of a circus performer who can defy gravity. The way I see it, it should instead be a kind of *roundedness*. We're always going to be not enough of one thing and too much of another, that's just the way it is. It's helped me to think of it less like a set of balancing scales that tips over when one side is too heavy, and more like a pie chart across infinite areas of our lives. The pie chart adjusts and readjusts daily, weekly, seasonally – but the important thing is that it all adds up to one big whole: our rounded life. As much as that sounds like the title for an insufferable TV show about a picture-perfect, Gwyneth Paltrow-headed family, I think there is a huge amount of value in viewing our life less like it's about to capsize one way or another, and more that it's readjusting, changing and varying according to our priorities and circumstances. I guess the challenge comes in avoiding this roundedness morphing into another expectation we can't uphold, and the way to combat that is to recognise that there is no single solution for each of us at any one time. The point of the pie chart is that the distributions aren't set in stone, and flexibility is valued over rigidity. It's in looking at the slices as boundaries rather than barriers, with governing values rather than strict rules, that we're able to get a realistic take of what we want our lives to look like. Hold this thought for a little while longer, because this is a key concept that we'll keep coming back to.

I've always had quite a stubborn view of work and rest. I don't know what hyper-disciplinary Miss Trunchbull lives in my brain, but there's a little voice there whispering that 'rest is for the weak', even though I *know* it's not (or that I'm allowed to be weak, regularly). I have to genuinely slap myself out of it when I'm in a rut or being harsh on myself, valuing hours worked over effectiveness just to prove to myself that I can do it. I'm genuinely the type of person that rejects 'The Hare and the Tortoise' story on the basis that *the hare would obviously win, it's a fucking tortoise!* I'd probably be the type of person who'd buy this book as a 'productivity blueprint', get to this section and slam it shut. I've learnt about productivity and work, haven't I? That's the important part, isn't it? The rest is just for people who can't stomach working the whole time, and I *can't* be one of those, can I?

What I've concentrated on teaching myself, and learning and unlearning again and again, is the interaction between working and not working – identifying when I'm genuinely being good at caring for myself by stopping work, or when I'm just being lazy. There are times when I find it really hard to navigate, and I think in part it's because of the way we view self-care as a generation, and in part just how some of us are wired. Self-care, much like hustle, has been blown out of proportion and turned into something floaty and incompatible with discipline and working hard. So let's bring it back to basics. Let's understand how we can make it *compatible* with our lives

151

and work, so that it's of value to us, rather than another buzzword we're not quite sure what to do with.

What I'm hoping to encourage is that you start to see self-care *as* productivity. Not as something you need to balance with working hard. Not just as facemasks and baths, saying no and cancelling your plans. But as actual 'I am taking care of myself and respecting my limitations' caring for yourself. Understanding yourself. Learning yourself. Mothering yourself. Respecting yourself. Whenever I find myself losing that, I take self-care back to its literal meaning: *caring for myself*. Something in which there is no right or wrong, or a commercialised entity that's being sold. It's just about making sure I'm getting what I need to be okay. We need to manage self-care as productivity so that it can be a *tool,* rather than an *excuse*.

People say that you can't pour from an empty cup, and it's true, but it's more complex than that. A cup doesn't represent our entire lives (also, who pours from a cup? *Surely* a jug would be more apt). We know we can't pour from that empty cup, but sometimes we don't know how to fill that cup back up. Sometimes the cup isn't empty; we just can't be bothered to pour, and the important thing is knowing when to pour, when to stop pouring, when to pour bolder and when to fix the cup itself. It's time to understand the benefits of hardly working, and the ability to incorporate stepping away from work as an *essential* part of productivity.

CHAPTER SIX

HAVING IT ALL

Since its introduction, the concept of 'having it all' has transformed almost as much as our opinions of it. In her 1982 book, *Having It All: Love, Success, Sex, Money ... Even if You're Starting With Nothing*, Helen Gurley Brown didn't so much as mention children. And yet, in the aftermath of its publication, the book was picked up, expanded, regurgitated and heralded as the birth of the idea that women could 'have it all' ('all' being a career and a family, of course). In its wake, the term became the poster child for women who were able to balance 'everything': being a good mother, having a high-flying career and a happy family life. Gurley Brown's discussions are more than a little dated now, and read as simultaneously quaint and eye-roll-inducing, but the book still stands as an important marking post in labelling the largely unreachable phenomenon that women still recognise today: how to deal with the competing pressures of our personal and professional lives and, crucially, come out on top.

I don't think that it's a push to say that in the generations since Gurley Brown, the ways in which we interpret and use 'having it all' have changed. In the forty years since it was first introduced, the concept has been vehemently rejected, ripped up and burned, and is now no longer even discussed as standard by Gen Z and beyond. It went from symbolising a feminist dream, to being used almost sarcastically as short-hand for a culture that encourages women to navigate across an impossible balancing beam in lieu of making reasonable demands on society that would make such a feat possible: equal pay, maternity leave and other equalising policies. But, in my generation, it seems the term 'having it all' is being reborn to expand beyond the sphere of gender inequality. We've generously built on the dilemma and begun to enforce it at a younger and younger age – a rite of passage that never ends. From school – with its redeeming extra-curricular features on top of compulsory work, the pressures of being popular, clever but carefree, and sharing the fruits of your popularity online – we've made the balancing act a life-long preoccupation, applicable to all. Much like an egg-and-spoon, sack and three-legged race all in one – a race that we're constantly urged to fumble through with unfettered enthusiasm as we progress in our lives.

I feel like there are two possible conclusions to be drawn from the fact that I'm sitting here – someone privately educated, who was lucky to have grown up juggling the expectation to achieve top grades while pursuing a range of extra-curricular activities and is therefore arguably primed for a life of balancing – and writing, concerned, about this transformation. The first one is that I'm just ungrateful – because who on earth complains about having *too many* opportunities, when so many people don't have any, rather than just enjoying my after-school basket-weaving class? And it may well be justified. But as I write this, screaming 'snowflake' aggressively at my laptop screen reflection, it dawns on me that this is by no means a problem faced only by privileged people who were encouraged to have their fingers in all the pies. Our world has transformed to *require* this type of breadth, not simply encourage it. Yet the reality of structural inequality means that some people are better equipped to deal with it than others: the greater the focus on extra-curricular activities, in school and at home, the more paths open up. I got through school (and university) on music scholarships, after all. Taking part in a variety of activities will mean that you develop a greater range of skills (which you can then show off on your CV), and it can also be an easy way to make connections that will serve you later on in life – and so the cycle perpetuates. It's vital that we make changes to arm everyone with the information and skills now necessary to aid success in their chosen field. To return to the race analogy, we're all competing in the crazy obstacle course, but some of us aren't given the spoon, or the sack, or the egg – and to me, that suggests this discussion is more important than ever.

In our move from only seeing small parts of other people's lives to seeing multiple people seemingly succeeding at multiple things, we've taken the concept of 'having it all' and multiplied it, squared it, added a few side-hustles and subtracted more reality. We want to balance more than ever, while also working more than ever. The two huge pillars of women's traditionally impossible work-life balance (progressing in their career and raising a family) have transformed and expanded to another (just as impossible) ideal: being able to balance work (which has expanded in hours and intensity) and life (which includes friendships, relationships, time to ourselves, going to the gym, looking nice, maintaining good mental health, and also being *seen* to be doing all of the above). The dreaded phrase 'work-life balance' does seem emblematic of where this whole conversation has taken us; it simplifies an enormously complex issue with a fraught and gendered social history into a reductive binary. It's an easily-said-but-impossible-to-actually-apply term. Having it all, to our generation, is less about women rejecting the constraints of a society not built for their success, and more about attempting to do everything all the time, excel at everything, have fun with everything, and sharing that constantly. And though it has expanded in form, it remains a concept weighted towards women. It is in our societally-imposed version of success, which is still contingent on being able to balance a relationship and family life with work, or it'll act as an instant antidote to whatever career-based success we've enjoyed. *'She's the best in the business! BUT she hasn't held down a relationship for more than a few months – I certainly wouldn't want that.'*

Think, for instance, of how interviews with famous women often seem to end up as a discussion of their personal life rather than their professional success. Cue Rihanna's memorable 'I'm not looking for a man, let's start there' in response to an interviewer asking her what she's looking for in a man, at her business collaboration launch. It seems almost trite to point out that the same questions are rarely asked of men. Questions posed to the Simon Cowells and Cristiano Ronaldos of this world (we'll call them the 'similar-net-worth-to-Rihanna' crew) focus on their latest business venture to capitalise on their growing fame.

What this showcases is the very real bias behind the idea that it's completely appropriate to ask men about the event they might be at, or the recent work they might be publicising, in interviews that are intended to be about their work; whereas women are tethered inextricably to the domestic sphere, and our interest in their professional lives is tempered by our need to see that same success paralleled in their personal lives. Perhaps we can fight this on two fronts: acknowledging such questions are inappropriate when interviewing women in a professional setting; and asking men about their families in professional contexts too, to encourage equal responsibility. At the very least, there is an uncomfortable parallel between these two situations and, even if not actively limiting women, it shows our continuing expectation that women should straddle both domestic and professional spaces. A woman's ability to 'keep' a home and her maternal qualities directly inform society's perception of her worth – and therefore her success.

Despite our progress (because don't get me wrong, we've come on leaps and bounds since Gurley Brown's time, when single women couldn't even get a mortgage), you can see women's anxious relationship with 'having it all' lingering on. It's worth noting that it is illegal to ask a woman about whether she plans to have children in a job interview, precisely because it has historically been grounds for discrimination (if we're also counting the present as history). Yet in a survey by the Equality and Human Rights Commission in 2018, 36 per cent of private-sector employers expressed the opinion that they 'think it's okay' to question prospective employees about their future plans for children. And a staggering 46 per cent of these employers felt it 'reasonable' to ask whether women have young children during a job interview. Other than raising an eyebrow at anything illegal being publicly described as 'okay', it needs to be questioned why employers would want to know the answer if they didn't also think it would disrupt a woman's work. (Unless, of course, they didn't just want to know whether the candidate had potential playmates for their own children, who had been finding it hard to make friends.) In that assumption, there is a silent recognition of the inadequate support structures we currently have in place to fight this inequality. Clearly, some employers aren't confident that you can 'have it all' in terms of work and family, and they may be right to an extent: it leads on to complicated questions around maternity *and* paternity leave, as well as the pay gap (does it make more sense for a woman to give up her job to provide care if the man earns more money? Or has this discrepancy arisen to begin with from the expectation that she would at some point have children? Perhaps we need to be looking to Scandinavia's famously progressive approach to paternity leave and childcare as a step forwards).

While it's still societally radical, as a woman, to suggest that you might not want children or not care about your career, it also seems radical to want both equally (cue 'I don't know how she does it', circa 2011). Meanwhile, it's radical that a man's idea of 'having it all' might be to realise his dream of being a house husband – raising children, baking bread and making jam while his partner brings home the bacon. The only truly radical attitude, however, seems to be the belief that everyone's 'all' is different: the assertion that it's defined on your own terms, and no one else's.

The whole premise of the book after all is that balancing work fulfilment and self-fulfilment *effectively* is crucial to our mental health and general wellbeing. It's not about having it all, it's about knowing what you want and when you want it and learning how to harness the merits of productivity and self-care alike – understanding you cannot have one without the other. To come back again to our machine metaphor, it's about moving away from treating ourselves as mechanisms and learning to appreciate our human complexities.

I wonder if the phrase 'having it all' makes this aim seem really demanding, and sometimes disincentivises us from making reasonable demands of our lives: if we want, and are in the fortunate enough financial position to do so, why shouldn't we aim to work four days a week and spend more time having fun with our friends and family? Surely that, too, is 'all'? There is a misconception in today's culture that there is a homogenous 'all' we're all chasing after, yet we're seeing more and more millennial women publicly declaring they don't want children, and an increasing number of people pursuing four-day weeks to create a lifestyle better suited to them. So if we want even a chance of having it all, we have to define what our 'all' is, rejecting its implications of smiling children and bustling careers, and everything else – unless that's what we want.

While I'd love to sit here all day discussing the historical and contemporary implications of 'having it all', it's perhaps more productive (in all senses of the word) to shift the focus on to how we can utilise this concept as a tool if we start thinking about it differently. I don't believe we should do away with the term completely – we do, after all, want both work fulfilment and self-fulfilment, and telling ourselves to just reject the idea of #balance and waft through life doing a bit of everything, or to concentrate on one thing as if we were a single-purpose kitchen appliance, isn't realistic either. For example, if you decide that you don't want a high-flying career or children, but do want a consistent job that provides for your needs, a buzzing social life, to keep fit and to spend a good deal of time with your family, you still need to figure out how best to fit all those elements into your life. But we do need to reject the idea that 'all' is everything, and replace that with the assertion that 'all' is everything we choose to want. And we have to understand that having it all, all of the time, is unattainable.

Think back to that adjusting, rounded pie chart, divided into our goals and desires. If you imagine fitting everything you want into this pie chart over a day, it sounds impossible; over a week, it sounds quite terrifying; over a month, it's beginning to sound fun and busy; and over a year, it no longer seems so daunting to include most, if not all, the things you had in mind. Having it all is ultimately a long game played out day-by-day in the form of self-actualising, and you need a bigger picture if you're aiming for fulfilment. It might not be a perfect work-life balance, and more a work-life-constantly-adjusting-distribution-of-time-dependent-on-a-lot-of-things, but the truth is we can all use some practical advice to help us maximise the enjoyment we get in our day, no matter what this mystical work-life balance means to you.

Pieces of the pie will come in and out (at your discretion and due to circumstances out of your control) and will inevitably adjust to constitute greater and lesser proportions of your life. When you're young and have no dependents, you might give more time to your career; and as you get older, and children, elderly parents or other responsibilities require more of your time, your pie chart will change accordingly. Once we've acknowledged this, we need to concentrate on practical methods to help incorporate a breadth of experience into our busy lives, where we want and need it. There's no point me sitting here – proud of the way I generally maintain things I love in my life pretty much regardless of how busy I am – and telling you it's impossible. Of course, I have no dependents, I am physically and mentally healthy, I am self-employed with every labellable type of mobility, and this may not be the same for you. Perhaps you have more responsibilities and duties in some areas, and less in others – I cannot tell you what you can and can't fit in. In order to utilise this concept to your own advantage, you have to figure out what your 'all' is at each moment and work accordingly, distributing your time to achieve all those things you want, while also enjoying those slices of pie that aren't part of 'success' but are high priority for happiness and fulfilment.

Let's take this pie chart that represents your life and all those parts within it, and remove the 'chart': here you have your life pie. It's made from the ingredients that together make up what you want your 'all' to be – you can't just keep chucking ingredients in and hoping for the best (tell that to Chef Grace); each one plays a role and they complement each other. It's all about deciding which ingredients we want our pie to be made up of (sounding weird yet?), how to practically fit all of them in, and maintaining that rounded approach to our lives. Solutions, not problems, pie people!

*

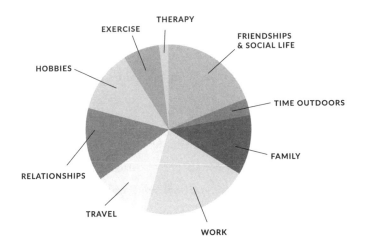

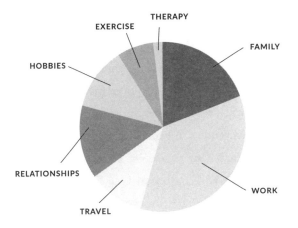

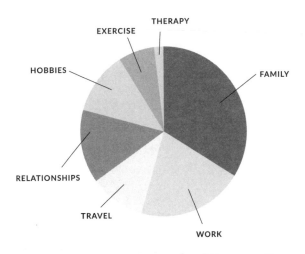

You might be thinking, 'Okay, but how is more planning and adding loads of things into my life self-care? Surely this is a recipe for burnout, not for a delicious life pie?' *Having* it all doesn't mean *doing* it all, and while we'll discuss this thoroughly in the next chapter, it's important that you bear it in mind before self-care becomes yet another part of the *more more more* mentality. There's a balance between tough love and really needing to sit back and do nothing, and that line isn't just on the edge of burnout. Self-care doesn't mean maximum enjoyment always, or trying to fit as many things as physically possible into your day until you collapse on the floor, but if you do want to fit different things into your life, you're going to have a better time if it's well planned. Things won't always just slot in on their own, and having structure will help you avoid feeling overwhelmed. If you're struggling with your mental health and feeling burned out, for instance, certain self-care practices – such as seeing a counsellor regularly – should take precedence if they're something you can afford, and prioritised over other less formal approaches. It might take some work, but once you master striking the right balance when it comes to structure, you're so much more likely to feel more fulfilled in your everyday.

First things first: you need to establish what ingredients are in your pie. (I'm a leek and mushroom gal myself.) This is *the* most important part of the process. A lot of the time, things we think are the 'most important' parts of our lives actually aren't a priority for us (just as relevant here as in Chapter 2) and that might be what's throwing us off our long-term goals or daily enjoyment. It's vital to get in touch with this and be clear on what *you* want to spend your time doing, versus what you might *think* you do.

For instance, you might think finding a romantic partner is a priority for you. Every time a friend can't hang out because they're with their SO, you might feel a little envious, or like that's what you're missing. But if you are signed up to a couple of dating apps and avoiding messaging anyone back, or turning down dates constantly, then maybe a relationship just isn't at the top of your list right now. Sure, this is a hefty dose of tough love – but trust me when I say it's going to be a lot tougher if you think dating is included in your 'all' when, deep down, you have a long list of other things you'd rather spend your time on. There might simply not be space for it to be a top priority, and that's fine as long as you let yourself accept it. Don't set yourself up for a losing battle chasing something that you don't even really want, at least not right now. It might be that some things need to take a back seat for a while, in order to get the 'all' that means more to you at the moment.

None of this is set in stone – it adjusts at your command, when you make a commitment and reflect that in your actions. We know now that it's not about having it all, all of the time; it's about figuring out what you do want and making *that* happen with a realistic oversight of your time and priorities. As we've touched on at various points, our goals and desires will ebb and flow throughout our life, and it's important to start valuing that fluidity rather than fighting against it.

Ask yourself the following questions to prompt your recipe creation:

1. What five things do you spend most of your time doing?
2. What one thing would you like to do more of?
3. Are the top five things you spend most of your time doing in line with the goals you set out for your success in Chapter 4?
   o For example, if you have a side-hustle and one of your goals is turning that into a full-time job, if it's not in your top five things you spend your time on, you might want to think about adjusting.

o Equally, address whether these are a result of *your* goals, or whether they're a result of the pressures we all have thrust upon us. Are you feeding your own dreams or those of the people around you?

4. What are the top three most important things to you in your life?
   o Is this reflected in question 1?

5. What are the things you keep putting off, and why are you putting them off?
   o Is it because you don't actually want them as much as your other pieces of pie right now, or is it because you need to re-evaluate how you spend your time?

After deciding what your 'all' is, you're going to need to plan how to fit it in. *I know*, it's tiresome even hearing the term 'time management' outside of working life – and you most likely already know the things you like to do and that make you feel good – but sometimes actively plotting this out does give you the knowledge and oversight you need to implement exactly what you want from your free time. It might seem like a chore, but I believe that it's such a privilege where we can do it: it's you taking control, being deliberate with your time, carving out and making sacred the space in your day for the things *you* want. The amount of time you have to play with and your flexibility within that will vary depending on your individual circumstances, but whatever your situation, it's an incredibly empowering thing to do and you'll be saving yourself so much grief in the long run if you create at least a loose structure. I'm not suggesting you go militant and give yourself exactly one hour forty-two minutes to have a drink with your friends, but you do need some idea of how you'll fit 'painting' into your schedule if that's important to you.

Sometimes you have to do a little bit of boring planning and time management to ensure you get the joy of *doing*. Hardly working is about being productive too, and the secret to having variety in your day isn't about having some superhuman amount of time, it's about making that time work optimally, or being selective with your priorities. One or the other. This really is the key to balancing everything, and the five minutes you spend on planning will bring infinite moments of joy and fulfilment from being able to enjoy things you love with goal-based priorities. Finally, it almost goes without saying that one of the most effective ways of fitting everything you want to do into your busy life is by making sure that the time you spend working is as productive and effective as possible.

It's up to you to decide what level of planning you go to – it's not necessary to plan your weekends meticulously, unless you have so many things in your pie that you'd rather do that than risk not fitting it all in. And it also doesn't have to be a one-size-fits-every-day plan. There might be times when you know that you'll go to the gym, or see your friends and family this weekend, but you also know there isn't a need to actively plan those by the hour and you'd rather enjoy the freedom. It's totally up to you. For me, when I want more things in my pie, I need to be clearer in my planning. If I want to reach my work-based goals and have dinner with the girls at least once a week, all while working out for my mental health and having some time to myself, I *know* I'm much better off stomaching the five minutes of planning and the feeling that I'm being OTT than spending the week feeling overwhelmed. The general rule is: more ingredients, more planning, more things fit in; fewer ingredients, less planning, fewer things fit in (and that in itself is self-care, too). That's just reality – and common sense. It's also worth remembering that putting in the energy to schedule something can start out as planning, but gradually becomes a habit. Actively ring-fencing time before bed to relax as part of maintaining good sleep hygiene might feel a bit forced to begin with (I certainly haven't aced it yet), but becomes more embedded in your routine as you practise it – planning is a habit that keeps paying off.

It might sound like I'm repeating myself, but I believe that the key to this all is setting boundaries and learning when to move them. I find that, with those pieces of my pie I generally enjoy less, I'm better off treating them more stringently. For example, I *love* the effect that going to the gym has on my mindset, and I care about my physical appearance and fitness. It's a priority for me, and I absolutely want it in my pie. But if I don't schedule in my gym sessions, I've got about as much hope of making them happen in my sleep as I do in my waking hours. That's because I still see exercise as a bit of a 'chore', no matter how much I love its effects. Talk about self-sabotage, eh? If I had to have a meeting but didn't schedule it in, I wouldn't find time or energy to make it happen – it would float around as a prospective calendar entry until we all just forgot about it, or pushed it back to 2052. I'm the same with the gym, because my mind clearly sees it in the same way as it sees work. So I schedule my gym sessions like I would a doctor's appointment. That way it's in my week and I know there's space for it (in the morning before work for me!), so I'm more likely to make it happen simply because it's scheduled.

It also creates a clearer boundary in my head, making it harder to procrastinate or push it aside if it's staring at me from my calendar.

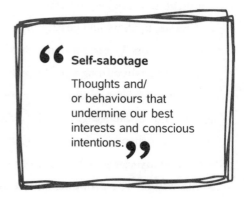

Self-sabotage

Thoughts and/ or behaviours that undermine our best interests and conscious intentions.

Now, even if you plan your balancing act to the max, you still might find it hard to fit in everything you want. I guess the best way to think of it is that you need clear, strong boundaries between different elements of your pie chart, but that you can move those lines, adjusting the time you spend on each thing, and changing up which elements come in and out. It's important to learn how to be flexible without being too self-critical. You need to understand that you can only fit a certain amount into your life at any one time. And one of the best ways to do this is by having visibility over your time. For example, you might look at your day one morning, knowing your life is 90 per cent work right now, and see your well-meaning gym class booking and dinner with friends that you put in last week before that last-minute deadline came in. You might genuinely want to keep them there, because you want to shift that proportion of work down, or it might actually be more 'self-care' of you to move your gym class and rearrange dinner from the off, rather than getting to the end of the day, still swamped with work and feeling flaky because you've had to cancel on your friend who's already at the restaurant, and you've missed your class (never mind the cancellation fee). The outcome is the same but the psychological effect is different – you move from a mindset of failure to one of awareness and adaptation – you're setting yourself up for success even though the end result of this 'success' is exactly the same as its 'failure' equivalent. That one change is the difference between you ruling your life and setting boundaries, and the things you're trying to balance towering over you.

Despite this, it would be incredibly naive of me to assume that we all have complete control over our own time, or even that we have a similar amount of control. I come from a position of huge privilege: aside from those I was born with, I'm employed by my own company, and while that comes with its own time challenges, it leaves me able to enforce certain boundaries I am very aware others aren't afforded the power to set, due to a combination of social and economic factors. There are many, many things that might stand in the way of you actioning any of this, with financial restrictions being some of the most pressing: having to work long hours or multiple jobs; struggling with mental health and lacking adequate support; not being able to afford accommodation close to work and having to rent far away with long commuting hours, for example. Some things will be non-negotiable, and will impact how much control you actually have over your day.

If you're twenty-one, with no responsibilities aside from those to yourself and a flexible working arrangement, any time spent not working is time you can control and spend on yourself. Alternatively, if you're a single mum with three kids working a shift job, not only does how 'effectively' you work not change your time commitment because you have hours you have to stick to, but you also have non-negotiables outside of work (feeding your kids, picking them up from school, the list goes on). It goes without saying that your pie is already fuller than mine, and while there's room for movement in some areas, there may not be in others – a lot of those lines *can't* move, and you can't remove the slices from the pie, so the amount of time you have to play with is different.

It would be ignorant (and quite insufferable) for me to sit here and say that's combatable when I haven't been in the large majority of those situations. But, as I said earlier, you have a duty to yourself to make active decisions about how you want your time to be spent *where possible*. There's a shift in mindset from one of feeling like your life is getting away from you, to acknowledging there are some non-negotiables but that you have power over the rest of it, even if you decide that that time is best spent resting and recuperating. I hope that doesn't sound sheltered, and I hope you can see where this could help, regardless of your individual circumstances.

What I would also say is that none of this matters if you're not being honest with yourself about what's realistic. You can't expect to fit everything in just because you wrote it in your diary (if only). If your weekend plans are to go out with your friends and do absolutely nothing else, then fine! But if your plans include going out with your friends and also having lunch with your mum the next day, you probably shouldn't be hanging out your ass on Sunday to the point you have to run to the bathroom after your main course and gag a little every time your mum asks how your weekend is going. Of course you *can* do that, you just might want to consider the reality first. It's inevitable that things will slip or that you'll misjudge the time or energy you have – that's part of being human! Be kind to yourself, learn from it, regroup and move on. We all do it. Setting yourself up for success isn't about beating yourself up if you miss the mark.

Finally, I want you to know that you can look at every single thing you want to do, planned pristinely within your colour-coded diary, painting the perfect picture of balance, and say: *fuck that*. Knowing *how* to balance these things is important; knowing that you can reject them at any point is even more so. The reality is, sometimes you'll be doing everything you want to: you're seeing your friends, excelling at work, sweating buckets in the gym and sleeping well. Hello, #self-care icon! And sometimes you're going to be shit at balancing balance. Sometimes your pie chart will look more like one big homogeneously coloured dot, because your life is that work-focused, or family-focused, or you're going through a stage of poor mental or physical health. It's important to know that you can wake up after an awful night's sleep, look at your perfectly planned weekend, with your pie chart fully aligned to your goals, and decide to sack it all off. You can wake up and not be able to face doing it, adapt, listen to your body and say, *thanks, but no thanks*. That is self-care, too. The idea is that we know how to maximise our time spent doing things we love. The power and self-care of this new definition of 'having it all' come from knowing how to balance all the things we want to do, and equally from deciding not to.

CHAPTER SEVEN

THE ART OF DOING NOTHING

We've talked about self-care as productive, goal-driven, fulfilling work in *Working Hard,* and we've talked about it in the form of doing a variety of things that you love outside of work, recharging through filling your life and having your 'all'. What we haven't yet discussed is self-care in its most commonly accepted form: stepping back, resting and doing 'nothing'. While it is by no means the only form of self-care, sometimes we just need to focus on *being* rather than *doing*. In order to 'have it all' for ourselves, we have to include within that the freedom to rest. Enter, *The Art of Doing Nothing* – stage-left, slightly late for its cue.

The 'having it all' concept, in its modern and morphed form, seems to have overlooked the fact that in order to have it all, we need to be able to do nothing – intentionally and often. As we've already explored, our very literal anxiety that time is money has resulted not necessarily in us using our time more wisely, but in a restlessness that means we must always be doing something to avoid being 'lazy'. I found it particularly enlightening (ha) to discover that Thomas Edison – father to arguably one of the most useful inventions, artificial light – is recorded to have been motivated to invent the lightbulb in order to spur on a 24/7 cycle of productivity. It seems that he believed people's lightbulb moments shouldn't be restricted by sleeping – and how better to liberate ourselves than by disrupting our natural circadian cycles? Clearly, it's not just Shiny Suit Twitter that tells us that 'while we're sleeping, the true winners are working' – the concept has infiltrated our wider culture, after years of incognito work. It's the reason why, as we've discussed throughout the book, we're seen as both the burnout generation and the snowflake, corner-cutting, lazy kids. We're either balls to the wall, monetising everything we do, or we're burned out and overturned, dead-bug style, on the sofa. The idea of doing nothing – as a neutral, planned, essential state – seems to have completely evaporated.

Looking around, in real life and online, I see two stereotypes of self-care: let's call them 'Wellness-Warriors' and 'Netflix-Zombies'. There's a dichotomy between these two accepted forms of 'what self-care is to us', and neither of them can serve our self-care needs in their entirety, or sometimes even at all. When self-care is presented as the pastel-hued world of wellness – a trillion-dollar industry fuelled by terms like 'mindfulness' – many people can't face or take it seriously. (I'm looking at you, vagina candle.) Meanwhile, we have a contrasting image of someone sitting like a zombie in front of Netflix, facemask on, scrolling mindlessly through social media, which isn't always the best way to recuperate either. It's no wonder we have these two competing knee-jerk reactions to hearing the term 'self-care' – that it's either a cult of indulgence or an indubitable waste of time.

What I want to talk about is *effective* self-care. An understanding that 'doing nothing' should not be the place we crawl to because of burnout, but an essential part of how we live, central to our productivity and both our working and non-working lives. The way I see it – and I'm dragging the machine metaphor back – we're more like an electric car than a petrol one (great for emissions too). We cannot be refuelled instantly and off we go again; we need to spend time recharging *before* we hit that 'Empty' mark in order to perform at our best. We need to reframe the way we see 'doing nothing' from a head-shaking stereotype of self-indulgent, time-wasting millennial bullshit, into something practical and useful – a way to recharge and reset productively. Unlike a parked car, we're never *actually* doing nothing: we're recharging, equipping ourselves with the energy we need to keep going. Our recharging isn't optional, it's essential. And often we'll plug in and recharge when we knew we'd need to, but sometimes we'll run out of charge sooner than we thought we would, just like our pesky electronics in the cold. If we don't engage in the concept effectively, we'll see it in the quality and quantity of our work, and in much more complex ways, such as our moods, self-worth and mental health – which is where the car comparison comes to a screeching halt.

One thing I find funny (read: ridiculous) is that it's now frowned upon in almost every industry to take a sick day *before* you're properly ill, even when you know that you're really run down and developing a cold. (Interestingly, I feel like I'm weak for even writing this, and certainly couldn't put money on *my* employees feeling like they could do the same, which is confronting. The thought of taking a day off due to being on the *verge* of a cold sits right next to 'taking a day off because your dog ate your report' in the things-you-just-don't-do-at-work pile.) Yet it stands to reason that if you spend just one day in bed resting, you'll be fine for the rest of the week. Instead, as is typical of our stoical twenty-first-century working culture, you end up waiting until you are actually quite sick and have infected the rest of your office with both a cold and your own glowing reputation of someone who just *does not take days off*. And when someone finally pleads with you to *just go home* (if you're lucky), you end up taking more days off while you recover than you would have needed had you fought it early. With the rise of the 'man flu' diagnosis arriving with the surprisingly brisk darkness of winter mornings each year, has come a culture which says that a cold is no justification to stay at home or to take it slower. It *must* be the full-blown flu or no dice! Perhaps this attitude might finally change in response to the 2020 pandemic as we all begin to fear *contagion* (and the embarrassment of spreading virulent disease) more than we fear the sentiment of looking weak and undedicated when a cold finally catches us.

In my first week working in a bank on a work experience scheme, I remember shadowing a relatively fresh Oxbridge graduate who got to the point of needing to take a toilet break every few minutes to eject the contents of his no-doubt-very-switched-on organs into the toilet bowl. I suggested (outrageously, I now realise) that perhaps he should go home for his wellbeing, and that of everyone around him. The scandalised (and very pale) infectee stared back at me wide-eyed, as if I'd suggested that he vomit on the lap of the office manager. He proudly exclaimed that he hadn't taken a sick day for the duration of his two-year grad scheme, and certainly did not intend to *ever*, because he wanted to keep his job. I turned my concentration back to my own screen in awe, and looked forward to my own stint as a corporate grad, where hurling into a porcelain bowl became the true marker of strength and ambition for my future.

Sadly, I don't believe our post-pandemic world will see a complete U-turn in our attitude to the sick day, and propose instead that we begin a three-tiered approach.

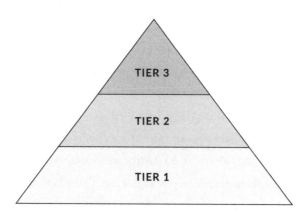

Tier 1: the 'come into work, but make it clear that if it gets worse, you intend to submit to a period of isolation'. It is vital at this stage to assure the team that you *certainly* won't be taking actual time off, oh for shame.

Tier 2: the 'stay-at-home work'. You are ill, but you will still work. The work will take place from home, as confirmed by your pre-pandemic stoicism; you *do not take days off,* but you are also caring and conscious of the processes of droplet infection. You will of course still have to demonstrate in some way that you *really are very ill,* in the form of a tactical thermometer-reading Instagram story, seeding out the information to those office-based followers and a stalking boss. If social media isn't your cup of tea, there's always the option of a very husky-voiced personal appearance on Zoom.

Tier 3: the unconscious, or hospitalised, not-working sick day.

I have presented this in a hierarchical format to demonstrate how unacceptable the actual non-working sick day will remain, especially given the proven science of working from home following pandemic life. But sarcasm aside, the point of this sick-day analysis is to highlight the importance of taking time to recuperate *before* it becomes urgent to do so – whether due to illness, burnout, or any other inevitable time-to-slow-down reality. As they say, a stitch in time saves nine.

As an entrepreneur who mostly delights in following other entrepreneurs on social media for inspiration and camaraderie, perhaps I'm hyper-exposed to the 'no days off' mentality. I've had to unfollow a significant number of people I genuinely admire because of the constant influx of 'no days off till it pays off'; 'let them sleep while you grind, let them party while you work' infographics graffitied onto my feed. When we follow stories of success, we feel both comforted and inspired by the supposed superhuman abilities of these people, which is perhaps why I also feel such pressure to publicise when I don't get enough sleep (apologies for past me, who starred in Chapter 5). I've come to realise that our 'no days off' mentality is a harmful glorification of burnout culture, where burnout is seen as some morally superior finish line coupled with a badge of honour. Sure, you can decide that you're better off not taking days off, on the rare occasion that's how you work best (spoiler: it's probably not), but you do need *time* off regardless.

To me, this mentality is a manifestation of a lack of boundaries between work and life, a lack of understanding of our human limits, and an inability to manage self-care as an important part of effective, good-quality work. You should be able to master the art of self-care in order to perform better in your 'days on'. Not letting yourself have days off doesn't make you a better, more productive person with robot-like abilities to work every hour of the day and never rest; it's a product of the line we've wrongly drawn tying together output, self-worth, success and unrelenting work. You might be able to work hard with longer-than-average endurance and produce a truly unbelievable amount of work, but here's the snag: if your limits – whatever they might be – are not respected, your quality of work isn't either.

We need to start valuing effective self-care as much as we do working while others sleep. It's not the route to success, it's the route to burnout, and it's not pretty.

This concept is among the most vital I've talked about in the book. Burnout isn't even really seen as a bad thing any more. I *hate* when people think I work all the time, and I *hate* when I have to tell them I don't and risk sounding lazy because of this culture we've created. Complaining because you *worked too hard for too long* and *everyone told you to stop but you just couldn't because you're so damn hard-working* is hardly seen as something to be ashamed of. But real burnout? It's harmful, unproductive, draining, terrifying, bad for your mental health. And that's what I know from hardly any time on this planet. Effective self-care – mastering the art of recharging – is the only way to avoid burnout, and therefore the only way to avoid being in that unproductive state, as well as being a brilliant way to look after your mental health. Once again: you don't need to choose between productivity and self-care, they are one and the same. Doing nothing is being productive, self-care is productive, even when it doesn't involve creating any tangible piece of work. I worry deeply that we, as a generation, won't be able to internalise this in the way we need to.

Let's change the rhetoric, for ourselves if nobody else.

'Fine,' I hear you say. 'But do we really need an entire chapter on doing nothing? Don't we all know how to do that already?' Bear with me: doing nothing isn't just about doing 'nothing'. It's an art, a skill. It's not just Netflix, essential oils and facemasks – sometimes it won't include any of those things. It's about engaging in effective and *necessary* forms of self-care.

The first rule of effective self-care is reflecting on what you *need* rather than what you *want*. There's just as much discipline in self-care as there is in productivity. Don't worry, I'm not going to whip out the planning stick again, but what I'm going to say next is important: we are not always the best at understanding our own needs, no matter how much we love a *listen to your body* graphic. Much to my dismay, we are not Sims with colour-coded Plumbobs that show us what we need. Self-sabotage is a very real danger when it comes to self-care, and it's sometimes hard to differentiate between 'being kind to ourselves' and good ol' procrastinating. As we know, sometimes the best way to care for ourselves is by being productive – finishing that brief, smashing something out ahead of deadline, because sometimes wanting to do nothing *is* a form of procrastination. But sometimes we really do need to step back and recharge. And while I can give you prompts to help you get to know yourself and your needs, at the end of the day we don't come with an instruction manual. There is no universal ideal ratio of time spent working vs doing things vs doing nothing or we'd be a lot better at balancing all three, and this book wouldn't exist. This is for you to experiment with in order to learn what works best for you. It's about trial and error, getting to know yourself, and not falling into a cycle of failure when you inevitably get it wrong sometimes. Learning what you need is about long-term reward rather than instant, short-term gratification, and it's often *very* hard to decipher. The over-arching blessing and curse of adulthood is that no one can tell you what's right for you. It will take time and effort to learn and implement, but it is the most important thing you can do for yourself, for your work, for your mental health and for your life.

The best way to start understanding your limits is by being honest and listening to your gut, and then learning from the outcome and doing it all over again (even if that involves never listening to your gut again). I know, for example, that I lean on the side of *work work work,* so if I think I need to do nothing, then I probably do. Alternatively, I need to take my instincts telling me to work more with a pinch of salt, as it might not always be what's actually best for me. Learn which side of the line you're on, and act accordingly. Similarly, I know that when I've been 'doing nothing' more than usual, I'm more likely to need an extra oomph to push me to take care of myself by getting back into my work. Sometimes, procrastination is your body telling you you need rest; sometimes, it's just procrastination. Go figure.

It might sound contradictory to advise you to 'listen to yourself', and also admit that 'sometimes you might not know yourself well enough, and therefore might get what you *need* wrong'. The reality is that, while we can and should work to 'learn' ourselves, we're also constantly evolving, and what might have been the answer once might no longer be appropriate. It's like attempting to learn a syllabus that changes every day. We can't get to a point where we 'know' ourselves indefinitely – what human can? – but it's likely that a level of self-awareness will spur growth elsewhere, and it's worth pursuing. At the end of the day, there's no concrete formula for the self-care we need; we're better off learning as much as we can and going from there, and adapting when that falls short or doesn't work in the way we thought it would.

Learning our boundaries means we can use them to our advantage, rather than see them as something that holds us back. When I was at university and work was particularly heavy, if I had one essay due on Monday and two on Thursday, I'd often work longer, more intense days at the beginning of the previous week in order to finish the Thursday essays way ahead of time and give myself a full week off. I know this sounds insane – how is doing an extra essay in a jam-packed week 'self-care'? She's a strange gal, our Grace. But this was a case of me knowing myself, and knowing that if I had something looming over me, I'd find it harder to fully relax (something I'm constantly working on). I knew that if I pushed myself harder for a concentrated period of time, I could have a full week to spend on other things I loved to do, as well as more time for 'doing nothing'. That, to me, was self-care in the midst of a packed schedule. It was creating, and adhering to, boundaries I'd put in place because I knew how I recharged best.

I also don't think it's about stepping away from just traditional work when we talk about 'doing nothing'. If I think about what drains me in my day-to-day life, work might reign supreme, but it's certainly not the sole contender. I often feel more drained after a ten-person dinner party than I ever do from an afternoon of creating a presentation, proving that there are many different types of 'work' pulling us in all directions. Just because something's not occupational, it doesn't mean it doesn't come with limits and boundaries. Doing nothing has to be about stepping back from social and emotional work too – relieving ourselves of the pressures of being a caring friend, a supportive partner, a good time, and anything else we're expected, and often want, to be. It's difficult, as we've discussed, to know when we'd be better off seeing our friends for dinner, or engaging in sweet FA.

Aside from 'learning yourself', you'll get some valuable tips from knowing whether you're an extrovert or an introvert, and where your emotional and social capacity lies. As a general rule, introverts tend to recuperate best on their own, and struggle to do so in social situations, whereas extroverts have a far greater capacity for social interaction, and a lowered need for alone time.

Interestingly, I've become more and more introverted as I've grown older, and this is something I've always associated with adult life and maturity. Perhaps this stems from looking up to those people who were happy in their own company, when I'd constantly need to be around others – entertaining, interacting, centre of attention. For me, 'growing up' was about getting comfortable with being on my own a lot of the time. When I moved to

London aged thirteen with just my mum, who worked or travelled most nights, I'd spend my time hopping round friends' houses, from sleepover to sleepover, never wanting to be home alone. I vividly remember one half-term holiday when I did not set foot in my own home once because I didn't want to be by myself. I went from friend A's to friend B's to friend C's and back to friend A's, with the single aim of not being alone. Truth be told, I didn't even really enjoy the company of one or two of these friends, but anything topped being on my own. It's safe to say that since then, I've worked tirelessly to change that, as it was more of a toxic, insecure trait than one based in genuine preference or emotional capacity.

As a result, I now have a real love affair with my own company, and have to coerce myself into seeing anyone aside from my own reflection on weekend nights – a true lover of extremes, me. In a complete 180-degree turn, now I have to question whether I'm due some of my own company or whether I'm shutting myself off from the outside world. And I've heard from introverted friends that they've experienced the opposite, as they've attempted to increase their capacity for social interaction. It just goes to show that to each is very much their own, and you may or may not want to increase or decrease your social capacity. Thanks to my impressive qualifications as absolutely-not-a-psychologist, it's clear to me that my introvertedness and extrovertedness fluctuate – from day to day, week to week, season to season. I find it's dependent on the moment, the people and myself – but, again, that's all the more reason to learn my patterns. You'll also get huge benefits from learning your friends' needs and preferences, too. I find friendships hardest when they don't understand that if I'd prefer not to do something spontaneously because I've booked in alone time, it's not anything against them, it's just what I need. I have friends I can chill with, and those I love to pieces but need to have the right amount of energy to see – we all know it's quite the minefield, but the more aware we can be of what we and the people around us need, the more we can incorporate this 'nothing' and recuperation into our lives and make *everyone* more happy and fulfilled.

I loved Caroline O'Donoghue's 2017 *Grazia* article titled 'Stop Pretending Your Flakiness is Self-Care'. It put a lot of the contradictions I'd seen surrounding self-care into very relevant words. Granted, a few themes in it may not run as well now, several years later (a softer explanation of the link between mental health and flakiness wouldn't have gone amiss), but the sentiment mainly stands. The article describes the rising phenomenon of cancelling on people as an act of self-care: we all do it, and it's hard to stop. But, O'Donoghue argues, the instant hit of endorphins as both parties agree to postpone (nearly always indefinitely) actually harms us in the long run. As with most instantly gratifying acts – pulling an unnecessary sickie included – the feeling is addictive. The sugar-high-reminiscent peak fades quickly into a trough of nothingness, and we find it hard to admit to ourselves that perhaps a little extra effort would've been the right thing to do. We'll never be able to decipher exactly what we need, all of the time, but with the right intention and enough willingness, we can grow to a point where, more often than not, we get it right.

Since committing to getting to know my own art of doing nothing, I have introduced it in my life in two (appropriately and professionally named) forms: planned nothing and fuck-it nothing. I believe we all need a mix of the two, though if you find it particularly hard to trust your gut, I recommend incorporating more planned nothing to begin with, as it's all about working it into your schedule and using it to learn about yourself, whereas it's harder to decipher when you actually need fuck-it nothing. For me, planned nothing comes in the form of weekends, and a certain number of evenings a week I keep free. My magic number is no fewer than two nights from Monday to Thursday kept entirely and non-negotiably to myself (as opposed to my mum's ability to spend every workday evening doing something sociable, then keeping the weekends pretty free – it turns out the magic number is certainly not genetic as her social schedule would make me explode). These conclusions are a result of having spent years establishing how much recharging I need, and then writing that into my schedule – while enviously side-eying my mother.

At the beginning of this year, I committed to taking weekends off for the first time since school. I've always had a variety of time-consuming things I do outside of work, meaning a weekend is never devoid of work or side-hustling. This was my first ever clear boundary, and I cannot tell you how much it's improved my mental health, creativity and quality of work. Initially, I thought it was a luxury I'd 'earned', and which would help me slow down overall, when in fact it is a boundary that has improved my quality of work tenfold. But there are endless other benefits to planning time off for yourself. I've found, for instance, that I always feel better during my planned nothing, because I'm in the mindset of having made a conscious decision to recharge in that time. It never feels like I'm procrastinating when I'm engaging in time off that I've planned and given myself permission to take. Fuck-it time off just won't give you that same relief of knowing you have that permission. In addition, you will find yourself working with that planned time off in mind, meaning you'll finish things in advance, and it's such a relief not having those tasks hanging over you. Parkinson's Law states that work will expand to fill whatever time you give it, so setting boundaries and having designated time off is important, for efficiency's sake as well as your wellbeing.

Having said that, both types of doing nothing are a condition of us being human, and we need to be able to know when to say *fuck it, I need a rest*. Fuck-it nothing is a failsafe, my safety net for when I didn't know myself well enough to plan accordingly, or when unexpected occurrences have zapped my energy. Any number of events can mean you just aren't at 100 per cent (or even at 40 per cent), and need to take time out. This form of nothing is about recognising that sometimes we don't get it right, or that sometimes life happens and you need to just 'fuck it' and do nothing. The extent to which you can exercise fuck-it nothing will vary wildly according to your circumstances – and for some people, being able to say *fuck it* may not always, if ever, be an option. Childcare, needing to work multiple jobs, the uncertainty that taking today off might mean you don't have a job tomorrow – there are many reasons why this isn't a luxury afforded to everyone all the time. I suppose, in these instances, it's about taking what you can – little, frequent chunks of nothing where possible: a thirty-minute break while a child is taking a nap, mindful lunch breaks at work – you'll know far better than I do what is available to you, but it's important to consider this and prioritise where possible.

Planned nothing is essential in our understanding that self-care is an indispensable part of our wider lives, and we can expect to have more and more fuck-it nothing if we don't plan well enough. But the truth is that fuck-it nothing is inevitable. We're complex, unpredictable beings living in a complex, unpredictable world (hello, 2020). You can't plan when you're not going to be able to work the way you want to. Most of my fuck-it nothing comes as a consequence of lack of sleep, mental health lows or unexpectedly low energy – a good example is almost every dinner out I've ever planned after a day of back-to-back meetings. And when I'm lagging, I can't focus or my work is taking much longer than normal, I know I need to just go 'fuck it, it's time to recharge', whether for half an hour or for the rest of the day. Of course, this is largely impossible with most jobs, mine included, so that's where planned nothing becomes even more important – the better I plan, the fewer lags I have. Fuck-it nothing is not as good for your mindset, because even if it's the right thing to do, it obstructs what you originally planned, and there's always a downfall to that. But when that happens, it's important to remind yourself that no matter how much you plan, those moments will always happen – it's just the way we, and the world, work. Learn from it, and be kind to yourself.

The second half of the effective self-care equation involves learning what those things are that recharge you. At risk of sounding like a broken record, this is another instance where the single most important thing you can do is really get to know yourself, in order to work alongside your needs and limits. I've found that I *never* know myself as well as I think I do, and I consider myself to be almost painfully self-aware. Often we don't even know what makes us feel shit, or we're aware of the things that make us feel good to begin with, but do the opposite after a certain amount of time. I'm not about to tell you to date yourself (although I believe in the concept more than I'd like to admit #mindfulness #selfhelp), but at least give yourself the time and energy to learn your likes, dislikes and limits, just as you would another person's.

Exercise

Carve out a double page spread in your notebook, and label one page 'Things that make me feel good' and the other 'Things that make me feel bad'. Then create a side heading for limits and exceptions, where applicable. I remember doing this when I decided to take a really pragmatic approach to making my life better and designing my work to be how I wanted it. Of course, we can't all base our lives entirely around things we love – often you just gotta do a spreadsheet, even if you *hate* it and =sum(headache) – but that doesn't mean we can't maximise these aspects of our lives where possible. Keep track of this over a fortnight or so to see what patterns emerge.

As an example, here is part of mine:

THINGS THAT MAKE ME FEEL GOOD	
	LIMITS & EXCEPTIONS
Seeing my friends for a drink or meal in the evening	When I have too much work or too many times a week. NB. Still feels good after a stressful day, as long as I don't feel too overwhelmed
Going on walks after work	No exceptions, should always be done or substituted for similarly wholesome activities
Having a chocolate bar at 3pm	Definitely no exceptions
Reading a book with morning coffee or on commute	A podcast is adequate substitution if my face is in someone's armpit on the underground. (Books, in such a scenario, take up precious personal space that's already being violated.)

THINGS THAT MAKE ME FEEL BAD	
	LIMITS & EXCEPTIONS
Eating pick-n-mix any time other than right at the end of the evening before bed (even then it gives me a sugar high and is not advised, but I know I will not listen when the giant strawbs are luring me with their sweet curves)	NB. NO EXCEPTIONS. You get grumpy
Having a long, heavy lunch in the middle of the work day	No exceptions, I cannot concentrate afterwards
Going on phone first thing in the morning	Only exception: when a risky text has been sent the night before and need to know if a reply has come in
Scrolling mindlessly on social media	Exceptions include: well-needed Netflix-Zombie state, when actually beneficial

Effective self-care is about knowing and responding to your boundaries, and being aware of how you feel when you reset by doing one thing vs another. Try to be disciplined about how you reset. Of course, this isn't always realistic and that's important to bear in mind. As an example, I know that I'll feel better after a stressful day if I see my friends (note to self: bookmark this list and look at it frequently) – there's nothing quite like taking the piss out of your day and seeing the humour in it while your friend rants about how Sharon stole another of her ideas in today's team meeting. And yet, when I'm feeling drained, the chances of me putting my big girl pants on and leaving the house are slim to say the least. Instead, I'll end up on my sofa in my sweatpants, scrolling mindlessly, with only a bag of pick-n-mix for sweet, sweet company. The reality is, sometimes you'll need to get it wrong over and over again until you start doing the right thing for you. Remember, the self-accountability vs self-criticism monitor? One alternative is getting your friends to hold you accountable where possible. I remember telling an ex-boyfriend about my mild pick-n-mix addiction, knowing that it was often *genuinely* the reason for my terrible moods and feeling low. I'd get to a lagging point in my day and reach for the sweets which, while great (sweets are fantastic, forget what your dentist says), would make me feel unbelievably shit once my sugar levels crashed. Having your adult boyfriend police your adult self on your pick-n-mix habit is, undoubtedly, a low point. But did it work? I can't promise it wasn't the reason for the relationship's demise, but absolutely.

One of the aspects of our 'off' time that we don't seem naturally equipped to confront is our social media usage. We discussed the attention economy way back in the Introduction, and it's an important point to consider too when it comes to self-care. After all, who doesn't Netflix-Zombie while scrolling mindlessly, with pretty much 'reward-seeking, lab-rat behaviour' – alternating between various apps, waiting for the next hit of something we find vaguely entertaining to make us let out a slightly-faster-than-usual exhale? It seems we all need to give more time to sussing out our own relationship with social media, and the way it makes us feel. Once we know where our limits lie, we can at least operate around them. Make social media better in how you treat it, and it will do the same in how it treats you.

Answering the following questions is a good start to working out where you stand:

1. How do you feel when you start your day by scrolling through social media?

2. How do you feel when you don't go on social media for a day?

3. Are there particular times of day where you're more likely to go on social media? How does it make you feel then? Able to escape, or anxious?

4. On a scale of one to ten, how much do you use social media as a procrastination tool?

5. How do you feel when you post on social media? Is that affected by the response you get to your post?

6. Do certain accounts make you feel bad about yourself? (Unfollow them, even if they're supposedly a 'healthy dose' of motivation. Spoiler alert: they're not. Motivating yourself by damaging your self-worth is borderline masochistic. You can always come back to them when you feel more confident.)

7. Write down three things that you saw on social media over the past week that affected how you felt.

8. What are your favourite parts of social media that add to your life beyond the app?

I'm of the opinion that we can have a healthy and beneficial relationship with social media, but that the large majority of us don't. Many of us seem to have a co-dependent relationship with it, and the less we allow it to escape beyond the realms of the apps themselves (affecting self-worth and changing how we attempt to appear to others), the better off we'll be. Don't let trying to control your outward narrative control you.

This is hardly going to sound like the most ground-breaking action, but I've found the small step of putting my phone away for a conscious amount of time per day to be immeasurably helpful. It sounds so insufferably Gen Z, but consciously implementing that behaviour – as someone who's grown up with its constant influence – has made a huge difference to everything from my mental health to my productivity. As I've said before, I rarely use my phone when doing any work other than admin ('Well Done of the Year' award presented to me, from me), but that's hardly the most wholesome activity. So when I take a walk at the end of my work days, I keep my phone in my bag rather than in my hand. (Incidentally, my sister read this passage and said I sounded loopy – who carries their phone in their hand anyway? I guess it really is a sliding scale of phone usage, and knowing where you are on that is the first step to knowing how strict you need to be with yourself.) Taking back control and showing yourself you can commit to that time apart is really important. If you genuinely don't believe you can do it, you might need to address your relationship with your phone and social media more urgently.

Being unable to stay away from something for even thirty minutes is an addiction. Confront it.

In Jenny Odell's *How to Do Nothing* – a powerful guide to resisting the attention economy – she mulls over Scott Polach's art piece 'Applause Encouraged'. In it, participants were admitted to an area to watch a sunset, with no phones or photographs allowed. As the sun set, the audience applauded. I mean, the fact that such an installation existed in the first place tells us a lot about our relationship with technology. I don't know about you, but I rarely see a beautiful sunset without whipping my phone out to photograph it. Now, I'm not one of those boomers (sorry everyone) that sighs at my generation's need to take photos of everything – I think that a lot of the time it allows us to immortalise beautiful memories. That being said, on the last holiday I went on – when I hadn't yet come across Jenny's book or Scott's piece – I had a similar thought, and decided to watch the sunset each night, no phone allowed. I wasn't expecting it to make a huge difference, if I'm being honest. But at the risk of sounding very woo-woo, there's a calm serenity you get from engaging with such a beautiful scene, and also from reclaiming power over your senses, which billion-dollar companies have robbed us of when they began fighting for our attention every second of every day. I'm by no means a full-time outdoorsy nature baby, but I do know that I feel happiest and least anxious when in nature, without a phone, yet I rarely allow myself enough space from all the work my phone brings in order to do that.

As well as analysing your relationship with social media, there are many other tried-and-tested methods of looking after yourself and your mental health. If you don't know where to start, these universal self-care rituals are great prompts. Much like our deep work triggers back in Chapter 2 – and pretty much everything in this book – some of these may work for you, and some might not. I'd also like to point out that nothing included below is particularly ground-breaking, and perhaps you do a lot of these things already. But I do believe that it's important to be reminded of the simple things, so that we can make a conscious decision to incorporate them more into our lives, rather than assume they will just happen on their own.

- **Move.** Move a little every day. You don't need to love working out, you don't even actually need to work out. You should, however, commit to moving your body in some way every day. Sitting in a chair to work all day, then transferring to the sofa for the evening is not going to give your body the stimulation it needs. Walk, exercise, dance, run, do yoga, cycle, take the stairs – just do *something*.
- **Leave the house at least once a day.** Even if it's just to go to the shops. The more time you spend in the house, the more you'll find it harder to leave, especially if you work from home. Cabin fever is *real*, and being aware of it is important, otherwise you might not realise what's happening.
- **Express gratitude.** You don't need to buy into the whole 'writing gratitudes' thing – it might be as simple as just saying three things you're grateful for in the morning as you wake up, or before you go to sleep. Understanding what you're grateful for can go a long way to allowing yourself to stay grounded and appreciative of where you are.
- **Eat nutritious food ...** Nourish your body and your brain with the vitamins and minerals it needs.
- **... but don't be too strict with what you eat.** There's more to life than calories, and you're hardly gonna look back in twenty years and wish you hadn't eaten that slutty brownie.

- **Connect with people.** Make an effort to connect with other people, old and new. You can decide how many and how often, but we do thrive off connection. Don't deprive yourself of that and close yourself off in busy periods.
- **Laugh often.** Commit to doing, reading, watching and listening to things that make you laugh. Seek the belly laugh. I still haven't got over my humour being entirely based around people falling over. It gives me the giggles.
- **Compliment yourself.** Tell yourself three things you love about who you are, every day. If you can't, ask people who love you, and then repeat them to yourself every day.
- **Sleep well.** You can't get the benefits sleep gives you anywhere else – you *have* to sleep enough, and the quality of your sleep matters too. A simple trick for better sleep is to avoid electronics for at least thirty minutes before bed. I know I've recommended it before, but read Matthew Walker's *Why We Sleep* for a deep dive.
- **Do good things for other people.** There's no such thing as a truly selfless act, because doing good things for other people makes you feel so good – a win-win!

You might look at the list above and see the big, meditation-shaped hole in it. I don't meditate, but I know people who swear by it. This might seem a little hypocritical; I mean, what is meditation if not 'the art of doing nothing'? I'm aware that the focus of this chapter and some of the other concepts we've spoken about through the book, including flow, echo fundamental elements of eastern religion and philosophy. But, while I definitely recognise the value and usefulness of concepts like mindfulness, which have developed from Buddhist thinking and practice, I've also seen a particularly commercialised side of meditation, and that makes it hard for me to place it outside of the Wellness-Warrior bubble. It's difficult to enjoy things when we feel they are being sold to us, but I think it's important to be able to adapt what's out there to make it work for us. My personal experience with meditation is, I'm sure, much like your experience with some of the things I swear by. The takeaway here is that everything is not going to work for everyone, so learn what works for you. I used to find the concept of gratitudes about as helpful as 'Live, Laugh, Love'-themed homeware, but I have since managed to extract what I need from the concept to make it work for me. Experiment with different techniques and keep a record of how each makes you feel, then you'll be able to create your own self-care rituals. The more time you commit to developing and understanding your relationship with these rituals, the more likely you'll have a successful relationship with keeping your sanity ship sailing through choppy waters. It's kind of like writing your *own* instruction manual.

The weekend before writing this chapter, I woke up on Saturday morning with a brain full of things I needed to action at work. Teams I needed to talk to, creative briefs I needed to change, and products I wanted to alter before approval. As I've said, my weekends are a no-go for work, so I found myself in a bit of a dilemma. It wasn't just inspiration that had struck, but also an anxiety that we needed to up our game – whole areas we needed to revamp in order to be where I wanted us to be. I was in two minds. On the one hand, I had a wholesome Saturday booked – a workout class followed by a drive to the countryside to walk with a friend and our dog children – and I had made a commitment *never* to compromise my weekends. Cancelling everything would definitely be something I'd regret in the hectic work week to follow, even though working seemed like the diligent thing to do at the same time. My brain was whirring in overdrive and I knew I wouldn't be able to enjoy the day with all of that in my head. I decided to go to my workout class and think about what to do while I was there – I definitely haven't mastered knowing what to do straight away, and I'm not sure I ever will. Throughout the class, I was able to calm my mind a little, ordering priorities and thinking about how I'd bring each point up to each team. Afterwards, I went home and wrote everything down in a structured way – what I wanted to change, where, and how I'd let people know on Monday. This sorting exercise did absolutely nothing to actually action my concerns, but did everything to soothe my mind. I was able to create a quick game plan, meaning I could then engage in my weekend of self-care.

There'll be times when traditional self-care won't be productive, and when your boundaries will coincide with bursts of inspiration or last-minute work overloads. We all have those days when it gets too much, and running a bubble bath would only make us drown in the stress. For me, writing down problems is one of the most effective ways to offload in those situations – keep track of your concerns, close in on the problem, then walk away. It's kind of like mini-therapy, except less expensive. On that Saturday, effective self-care was not simply pushing my concerns and ideas to the back of my mind and just going on the walk – but it also wasn't bailing on my walk and working all day (which would've been the result if I allowed myself more than thirty minutes with that pen and paper). Sometimes you need to listen to your body *and still* obey your boundaries, and the good news is, it's often possible to do both. Plus, when I came back to those notes on Monday, I realised I would've sounded insane if I'd sent my frantic, unordered concerns to the team in the moment. In reality, I needed time to mull over the situation, my intentions and game plan – by Monday, only about half of my original concerns actually needed to be dealt with. The others were on various roadmaps to be improved at later, more suitable times. My suggestion is, when it all gets too much, write it down, offload, create a vague plan of action, then leave the problem there and come back to it when you are next planning to work, or you'll spend your life cancelling plans to make sense of every single brainwave.

When it comes down to it, there's never going to be a foolproof method for deciphering with perfect accuracy when to do something and when to do nothing. We're not straightforward, and sometimes it's impossible to tell whether what we want and what we need are the same thing, or whether we're self-sabotaging. The art of doing nothing is a necessary ingredient in living a happy, successful and balanced life (even if those last three adjectives are hard to write in a sequence without feeling like I'm selling a three-day juice-cleanse retreat). For as long as we continue to categorise self-care as either a cult-like movement or a complete waste of time, we're never going to be able to use it effectively. The secret sauce lies in ignoring the noise made by these two competing mindsets, and getting to know ourselves and our own needs, knowing what makes us feel good and implementing that as much as we can. It's knowing that sometimes we'll feel good recharging on the sofa, sometimes what we really need is a long chat with our best friend, and sometimes we'll feel best if we push further into our work. But what we can never expect is to steer our working lives effectively towards success without accepting doing nothing as one of our basic needs and greatest strengths. We cannot create a game plan towards success while ignoring the fact that we're human beings with limits, and we can use those limits to our advantage. We need to practise and experiment and try different methods, then see what works for us so we can treat our work and our wellbeing with respect and care.

Self-care comes with tenderness and love for yourself, knowing you have flaws and knowing that's okay. You can attempt to work around them, and sometimes you'll fail – denying that is denying your reality – but at the end of the day, self-acceptance and maintaining self-worth is the most important form of self-care. You have to handle self-care with care – in the same way that we're not productivity machines, we're not self-care machines. If you get to the end of a busy day and engage in ineffective care, that's okay. Learn, implement, get it wrong, go again, and realise that this is just how life works. The sooner we accept that, the sooner we'll be accepting our own limits. That's what allows us to move forwards.

FINAL THOUGHTS

When I first decided to write this book, I honestly had no idea what it would entail. There's a huge amount of chatter online, in books, in studies, about our generations; I'm often asked to speak about it in my day job, especially when it comes to 'how to market' to Gen Z. The way we're talked about – having been born into an era of recession, technology and apparently avocado toast – it's as if the world birthed a new generation of bright green children. We're looked at with an eye to what on earth we're going to become, whether we're going to survive the climate crisis, whether we're a whole different type of human thanks to the alarming rate of technological advancement defining our every moment. Yet of all the dialogue surrounding the new working world, there is very little that has actually spoken to me and encapsulated what it is to be a part of this time. So I didn't even know where to start. For me, this book had to be as much about self-discovery as it was about imparting what I already knew.

So I began this deep exploration of myself – what I want, whether I really want that, what that's influenced by, *why* I want it, and how all of the above are affected by where I am within society and our current working landscape. I had some significant hiccups along the way – I mean, how can I evaluate the problems with our generation's working expectations when I benefit directly from them? Is it fair to create a productivity blueprint when I have entire teams working on every project I begin, and almost infinite outsourcing power? Is it inspirational to hear someone like me talking about working culture when I'm in the position I'm in, or is it just really fucking annoying?

And then, as I confronted all of these issues and cathartically wrote down my own evaluation of what I had the right to talk about, I started to realise that, even if you disagree with 99 per cent of the shit I say, at least you *know* you disagree with it. The problem isn't the content of the discussion around our generation, it's the lack of authenticity that is allowed to be heard *from* this generation. It's people talking *about* us all the time, so that we formulate opinions of what it's like to be part of this generation and this working world without even knowing what we think ourselves. We are being inspected from all angles, binoculars out, waiting for the whole of Gen Z's age bracket to join the workforce, to see what we're *really* like, whether we can *really* work or whether all we know are TikTok dances. We're allowing ourselves to be told who we are and what we want, and letting that speak for us before we even know what we want to speak about ourselves. But we have every right to reject this rhetoric, to clarify how we work in this world of interconnectivity and distraction, to redefine what purpose and productivity and everything in between means to us.

Instead of accepting these stipulations as truths, we little green children can throw it all in the bin and start again, picking and choosing what resonates for us and, in doing so, rewrite the dialogue for ourselves. The world has changed immeasurably over the past twenty or thirty years, and we don't need to take anything as given: we have the power to call this a blank slate *because* of all the changes we've witnessed. And we have it in us to write our own story. Individually. It's no one else's job, and the sooner we take that upon ourselves, rather than adopting blanket statements pressed upon us by today's world, the closer we'll be to understanding who we are and what we want.

I also want to stress that not one bit of any of this matters if you can't respect and accept yourself. You can have the best 'productivity method' in the world, get everything done all the time, become the epitome of efficiency and balance and effectiveness – but all of that will be meaningless if you don't allow yourself to respect what you want and need, and who you are. Over the course of this book, I've tried to instil the importance of that above all else: productivity is nothing without self-care; work is nothing without rest and recuperation; success is nothing without your own acknowledgement of how far you've come.

In the past year, I've struggled with self-love more than ever before. It's not that I don't think I'm worthy of love, or that I'm a bad person, but it's been a constant challenge to accept where I fall short of others' expectations – whether that's family, relationships, friends, or millions of people online. I made the decision, about two years ago, to begin the transition to creating longevity for my career that didn't involve sharing every moment of my life, all the time. I realised that my joy came from head-down work and building my brands mostly behind the scenes. While I loved – and I *really* loved – the sense of community I'd created in my audience, sharing what was going right and what had gone wrong *again*, I realised that I'd replaced a lot of my own internal self-worth and acceptance with external validation. I hadn't meant to, and if you told me that I had at the time, I probably would've argued my case to the ends of the earth. But the reality was that I'd started to grow on social media at a time when I was incredibly insecure. I didn't necessarily like who I was – how competitive I was with others in my own head, how I'd never been the best at anything, how I had this *longing* to be liked and accepted and found it embarrassingly hard to take any criticism. I was a teenager and it was natural, but I remember my childhood best friend sitting me down one day after another session of trying on clothes that led to me picking apart every element of my existence. She said that all my self-hatred and criticism were starting to project onto other people, and that I couldn't expect to accept myself – or for anyone else to accept me for that matter – if I spent my entire life expressing disgust because I didn't look nice enough, or perform well enough, or get the best grade, or wasn't the top choice. And she was right.

Soon after, I thought that by some miracle I'd overcome my overwhelming insecurities and was enjoying a fast-track ride all the way to mystical self-love. Only over the past year have I realised that rather than a healing process, I had covered up my insecurities with an external validation-shaped bandage. I've never admitted to this because I find it confronting. I find it so quintessentially Gen Z that I replaced an important, uncomfortable part of my growth with acceptance from others, and my own acceptance only came after that. When I decided to unknowingly take that bandage off, I found myself back at square one. I think the idea of self-love is strange (and certainly not British), because while I'll back myself to the end – I'll stand up for myself, assert my strengths, happily prove people wrong – there's still this underlying self-acceptance missing. It's not just about thinking you're great or appreciating your strengths or ignoring your downfalls; it seems to me to be this ineffable magic ingredient that is so hard to source and maintain. And I'm on the journey to get there as much as you might be. Some days I think I'm there, on others it's clear I'm really not. It fluctuates, ebbing and flowing on the sands of self-acceptance, but I finally know how important it is. I know that it's not optional – you have to accept yourself; in fact, it's the springboard to making everything else in this book work.

As humans we want to be liked – some of us certainly more than others. It's a natural part of our evolutionary biology: we want to be accepted into the pack. But now, more than ever, it's also irrational. We're bombarded from all angles with unsolicited opinions, but we're far from equipped to deal with that information. It's remarkably easy to replace internal validation with a desire for external approval – in fact, I think we've got to the point where pretty much all of us do. We've moved online, and whether it's our latest piece of work, our promotion or how we spend our free time, there's suddenly something lacking for most of us if that's not celebrated by others too. Sure, there are people who don't use social media, and I'm sure I'm at an extreme end of the spectrum, but the possibility of being accepted constantly, consistently and continuously beyond our everyday circles has implications on where we seek that self-worth.

I know that wanting to be liked by everyone is irrational and when I really think about it, I don't even think I *do* want to be liked by everyone – I certainly don't like everyone I meet or see online – and yet I'm affected when I know that people don't like me. It affects my self-love. But what I've slowly come to realise is that it's not always about self-*love*, but rather an unconditional self-acceptance – not devoid of accountability, or blind to improvement, but an acceptance of who you are regardless of your flaws. Sometimes it's even going to be a sort of neutrality towards yourself and your downfalls. I think that's why I find the self-love rhetoric tough to grasp sometimes – I'm not going to skip the gym for the third time in a week, or complete only half of my to-do list because I've been distracted by something far less important, and respond by staring my mirrored-self in the eye exclaiming *I LOVE YOU!* No matter how much you love other people in spite of what they do or where they fall short, you're always going to be harsher on yourself. That's why it's so much harder to give the love to yourself that you give so freely to others. There's no such thing as internal rose-tinted glasses. But there's also no point spending your life side-eyeing yourself and the mistakes you make – it certainly isn't going to help you improve. I used to have such a harsh attitude when it came to my standards for where I wanted to be. I used to believe that criticising myself internally and with constant self-deprecation was the antidote to every wrong turn, every mistake. And then I realised that it really isn't – it's unproductive and unnecessary. Self-accountability, where you take responsibility for your actions and decisions but leave judgement at the door, is infinitely more effective than self-criticism, every day of the week.

This self-worth is the most important thing you can develop for yourself, that any of us can develop. And it can't wait until you reach your goals. By its nature, it has to be embraced in spite of whether you reach them – and maybe you won't actually reach them without it. I'm not sure it's possible to fully experience success if you leave out your own self-worth; without it, you'll never *allow* yourself that feeling of success. It'll be up and down, and that is perhaps the most defining part of life, but you need to have an unconditional, underlying understanding that you're worth it (and not just as part of a L'Oréal ad).

I'm not telling you to settle, short of where you want to be, accepting a half-baked version of your dreams. What I'm talking about is accepting that you're on a journey, and you're not going to get there overnight. Sometimes the trajectory changes, sometimes it takes a U-turn and recalibrates, and sometimes you're going to have to try over and over again to make something stick. But allowing yourself to embark on that journey to reach your ambitions – in your career, your habits, your relationships – is one of the most effective forms of self-acceptance, and a powerful acknowledgement of your own self-worth. You can't expect to improve if you're not allowing yourself the love and acceptance you need to grow, even if you haven't quite made it yet. You need to accept and believe in who you are now, in order to trust that you have the capacity to get to where you want to go. If you don't genuinely believe in yourself and in your abilities, then how are you supposed to keep going? And, similarly, without that acceptance that this is where you are today, how are you supposed to chart a realistic path to get to where you want to be tomorrow?

The idea of self-worth underlines everything else in this book. When you develop self-worth, you develop self-accountability, self-acceptance, and an understanding that you owe it to yourself to create the life you want. In order to make any of this happen, you need to check in with yourself, again and again: whether that's recognising that you need to work harder, or that your work won't be enjoyable until you improve and take on extra bits here and there, or that your current productivity method revolves around pushing yourself to burnout then spending days recuperating, rather than respecting your own limits and boundaries. You might want – and need – to sit back sometimes, and we know that's not only okay, it's *essential*, but you need to learn your own boundaries and put them in place. And the only suggestion I can make is to evaluate and re-evaluate what you want in order to give yourself the chance of getting there. Have the discipline to make things happen, and to fight for where you want to be and how you want your life to make you feel, no matter what obstacles stand in your way. You can't expect things to change straight away, and you certainly can't expect them to change if you don't take the time to acknowledge them.

I've often felt lost. I think I've always imagined coming out of a fog someday and it all being clear – my path to success, self-love and acceptance from others and myself – but I've realised that this isn't going to happen. I cannot control outcomes. I cannot determine the future. The one thing I can determine is where I am, what I'm doing and what I attract. Self-actualising is now my constant goal, because it's the tool that I genuinely believe will lead me to where I want to be. Not in a chanting-round-a-fire way, but based in intention, in placing myself not on a path that is laid out for me, but on one that I'm clearing for myself. The ultimate goal is in the moment, in the journey, in intentionally revisiting and realigning every day to be self-actualising.

So what's next? Well, I want you to talk. I want you to discuss. I want you to disagree with me to your friends. Start the conversation, get comfortable with being uncomfortable and navigating this life with the people you love. There's no right answer. Just promise me one thing: that you'll talk about these issues once you've turned this final page, that you'll deep dive into your life and those of your friends. Get off your phones at dinner, take a second out of the gossip and talk about what makes you happy, what makes you feel lost, and where you want to be heading. And I promise, no matter where that is, you'll be able to create a path to get there.

ACKNOWLEDGEMENTS

To my editing team, who deserve the biggest acknowledgement of all.

To Abi, for spurring on much of the motivation for this book; for cultivating my endless streams of consciousness into something of value; for sharing your insultingly intelligent insight throughout the writing process. And to you and Megan for supporting me in pitching a book so far away from anything I've done before.

To Alice, for being the sister-editor hybrid from heaven. For your endless hours spent rationalising my thoughts, and for giving me a much-needed confidence boost after so many months of writing. Working with you has been like working with a really, really good version of my own brain, with a lot more information in it. I have loved every second of it.

To Anna, my editor at Hutchinson, for being there through every step of the writing journey. For encouraging me to write as myself, rather than anyone else, and for making my ten-minute voice notes into something worth writing about. For reassuring my ever-rising stress levels, for working around my rigid working patterns, and for listening to my every concern.

ACKNOWLEDGEMENTS

To Hutchinson and all of Penguin Random House, for supporting this book in every way possible, for allowing my mind to run free on a topic seemingly so far from my expertise, and for putting your confidence in me to partake in this incredibly important conversation.

Without all of you, this book would not have been possible, and my brain would still be an insurmountable jumble of nonsensical thoughts.

To my friends,

To Steph, for being so constantly and beautifully vulnerable with me, for giving your raw insight and for allowing me to have conversations with you that I wish I could have with myself. You inspire me every day.

To Alisha, for being my number one since day one. For allowing me to be your best friend and for understanding me inside out.

To Tom, Megan and Emerald, for making me beans on toast when I take none of my own advice and work until I forget what food is. For handing me a glass of wine when the day never seems to end. For allowing me the space I need to write, while locked in the same house, but simultaneously always being there when I need you.

To Bron, for sharing your unmatched intelligence and insight on some truly awful first drafts, and for helping me deal with my full-blown meltdown just a month before this book was due. Thank you for being there.

To Tiff, for being the best friend I never knew Ziggy needed and allowing me to escape to an endless stream of cafés to get this written, and for being there when I got home. I forgive you for usurping me in my dog's love. I understand you are soulmates.

To everyone at Oxford, for giving me the university experience I needed, despite me doing everything in my power to grow up faster. For teaching me what it is to never ever be close to being the cleverest person in the room, and for starting my obsession with reading things I could never begin to fully understand.

To Alicea, Sarah and Verity, for being my constant cheerleaders, right from the beginning. For helping me believe in myself and for bringing my ideas to life better than I ever could alone. For keeping the ships going no matter what crazy ideas I pursue, for the late nights, and for sharing such generous feedback on my writing.

To Alex, for enlightening me with your incredible work ethic and calm direction. For being an inspirational leader and for helping me through every second of the past few months. It's been short so far, but it's been very sweet.

To Shan, for seeing my potential long before I did. For matching my enthusiasm for work and growth and for constantly pushing me to be better. I hope you'll forgive me for dismissing hustle culture.

To Lexi, for walking into my life in February, looking as glamorous as ever, and for changing everything. You have transformed my ability to do every facet of my work, and have been a constant friend to me through every (frequent) bump in the road. Working with you is an endless pleasure, and all that I do is only possible because of your support, love and friendship. I thank my lucky stars every single day for you.

To the teams at TALA and SHREDDY,

For everything you have done to take these companies to where they are today. For accepting my sometimes less than traditional leadership style. For executing to perfection, and for growing with the brands from tiny ideas to incredible businesses. I hope you're as proud as I am of what you've achieved.

ACKNOWLEDGEMENTS

To my family,

For teaching me pretty much everything I know. For constantly keeping me grounded and for teaching me to challenge everything I see. For being more intelligent than I could ever try to be, and for being nice to me when I made that really bad Play-doh sculpture.

To Violet, for being my best friend for so many years, and for never letting me go un-checked up on. For knowing me inside out and for somehow always being there when I need you, no matter what.

To Flora, for teaching me so much about being myself, and for showing me how to live life on my own terms. For being so fiercely intelligent, and for showing me how to never let anyone question me.

To Alice, again, for being the most powerful older sister anyone could ever imagine. You are a powerhouse.

To my mum, for teaching me everything just by existing. For showing me that there is beauty in being exactly who you are, just by being your wonderful, quirky, hilarious and powerful self. For demonstrating the unmatchable brilliance of being a working woman, and for never letting me rely on anything other than myself. You taught me to be me, by being you, and it's an honour to be told I'm just like you, even if that's sometimes what makes us argue at Christmas. Your complete and unapologetic embracing of your selfhood has inspired me beyond anything else, and everything you have done has paved the way for everything I hope I will one day become.

To my dad, for being my rock before I even knew it. For giving me an insatiable appetite for achievement, evolution and success. For empathising with the downfalls of that very appetite and for imparting on me your invaluable wisdom. I'd never called you desperate for help before this month, and I have no idea why. You have been everything I've needed, and I couldn't have got through this year without you. I am incredibly lucky to have you, and I'll give up my stubborn independence every day if it means that I can work and live with someone as wonderful as you.

And lastly, to everyone who has ever supported me online, often more than I've supported myself. For allowing me to thrive and to grow into myself. For being here through each and every U-turn, and for helping me to aim for the best version of myself, then for supporting me when I fall short.

READING LIST

Reading is one of my favourite forms of self-care – as one of the only activities that truly allows complete mental escape from the outside world, it's my number one flow. But, like other things I perceive as a chore, I still have to discipline myself to actually *get* reading.

Last year, I began to realise how detrimental my morning social media consumption had come to be, and how it instantly dulled my creativity and enthusiasm for the day ahead. I found it daunting to constantly have a 'business' book on the go, and I started compiling online resources at the beginning of the month so that I could just pick up an article each morning to read with my coffee. Groundbreaking? Not at all. But it got me back into reading, and giving myself permission to dip in and out of books rather than feeling like I had to read them cover to cover made it seem a lot less of a chore.

Now I have a few books on the go at once to satisfy the different kinds of escape I'm after – sometimes, I want something heavy and highly educational; sometimes, I want a light-hearted opinion piece.

Here are my favourite resources for finding those articles and books I've particularly enjoyed. Add your own industry resources, and watch the depth and breadth of your knowledge grow!

Books

Business, Self-Development and Big Ideas

- *Atomic Habits: An Easy & Proven Way to Build Good Habits & Break Bad Ones*, James Clear (2018)
- *Big Friendship: How We Keep Each Other Close*, Ann Friedman and Aminatou Sow (2020)
- *Black Box Thinking: Marginal Gains and the Secrets of High Performance*, Matthew Syed (2015)
- *Can't Even: How Millennials Became the Burnout Generation*, Anne Helen Petersen (2021)
- *Deep Work: Rules for Focused Success in a Distracted World*, Cal Newport (2016)
- *Difficult Women: A History of Feminism in 11 Fights*, Helen Lewis (2020)
- *Digital Minimalism: Choosing a Focused Life in a Noisy World*, Cal Newport (2019)
- *Find Your Why: A Practical Guide for Discovering Purpose for You and Your Team*, Simon Sinek with David Mead and Peter Docker (2017)
- *Flow: The Psychology of Optimal Experience*, Mihaly Csikszentmihalyi (1990)
- *Freakonomics: A Rogue Economist Explores the Hidden Side of Everything*, Steven D. Levitt and Stephen J. Dubner (2006)
- *Grit: The Power of Passion and Perseverance*, Angela Duckworth (2016)
- *How Do We Know We're Doing It Right?: Essays on Modern Life*, Pandora Sykes (2020)
- *How to Do Nothing: Resisting the Attention Economy*, Jenny Odell (2019)
- Any of the Merky Books *How to …* series. At the point of compiling this list, the books in the series are: *How to Build It: Grow Your Brand* (Niran Vinod and Damola Timeyin), *How to Change It: Make a Difference* (Joshua Virasami), *How to Write It: Work With Words* (Anthony Anaxagorou), *How to Calm It: Relax Your Mind* (Grace Victory), *How to Save It: Fix Your Finances* (Bola Sol) and *How to Move It: Reset Your Body* (Joslyn Thompson Rule)
- *Lean In: Women, Work and the Will to Lead*, Sheryl Sandberg (2013)
- *Little Black Book: A Toolkit for Working Women*, Otegha Uwagba (2017)
- *Me and White Supremacy: How to Recognise Your Privilege, Combat Racism and Change the World*, Layla Saad (2020)

- *Mind Over Clutter: Cleaning Your Way to a Calm and Happy Home*, Nicola Lewis (2019)
- *ReWork: Change the Way You Work Forever*, Jason Fried and David Heinemeier Hansson (2010)
- *Self-Care for the Real World*, Nadia Narain and Katia Narain Phillips (2017)
- *Start With Why: How Great Leaders Inspire Everyone to Take Action*, Simon Sinek (2011)
- *Superfreakonomics: Global Cooling, Patriotic Prostitutes and Why Suicide Bombers Should Buy Life Insurance*, Steven D. Levitt and Stephen J. Dubner (2010)
- *Taking Up Space: The Black Girl's Manifesto for Change*, Chelsea Kwakye and Ọrẹ Ogunbiyi (2019)
- *The 4-Hour Work Week: Escape the 9–5, Live Anywhere and Join the New Rich*, Timothy Ferriss (2007)
- *The Happiness Trap: Stop Struggling, Start Living*, Dr Russ Harris (2007)
- *The Little Book of Talent: 52 Tips for Improving Your Skills*, Daniel Coyle (2012)
- *The Panic Years: Dates, Doubts and the Mother of All Decisions*, Nell Frizzell (2021)
- *The Productivity Project: Proven Ways to Become More Awesome*, Chris Bailey (2016)
- *The Working Woman's Handbook: Ideas, Insights and Inspiration for a Successful Creative Career*, Phoebe Lovatt (2017)
- *Too Fast To Think: How to Reclaim Your Creativity in a Hyper-connected Work Culture*, Chris Lewis (2016)
- *Trick Mirror: Reflections on Self-Delusion*, Jia Tolentino (2019)
- *Unfinished Business: Women, Men, Work, Family*, Anne-Marie Slaughter (2015)
- *Use Your Difference to Make a Difference: How to Connect and Communicate in a Cross-Cultural World*, Tayo Rockson (2019)
- *Whites: On Race and Other Falsehoods*, Otegha Uwagba (2020)
- *Who Cares Wins: Reasons for Optimism in Our Changing World*, Lily Cole (2020)
- *Why We Sleep: The New Science of Sleep and Dreams*, Matthew Walker (2017)
- *Work Rules!: Insights from Inside Google That Will Transform How You Live and Lead*, Laszlo Bock (2015)

Memoirs

I only really got into memoirs and autobiographies this year. I must admit, I had a misconception that they'd all be, well, dry – and not really something I could find myself getting lost in. How wrong I was! These are some of my favourite autobiographical books – from the funny, to the poignant, to the downright heartbreaking.

- *Becoming*, Michelle Obama (2018)
- *Everything I Know About Love*, Dolly Alderton (2018)
- *How To Fail: Everything I've Ever Learned from Things Going Wrong*, Elizabeth Day (2019)
- *Minor Feelings: A Reckoning on Race and the Asian Condition*, Cathy Park Hong (2020)
- *More than Enough: Claiming Space for Who You Are*, Elaine Welteroth (2019)
- *Priestdaddy*, Patricia Lockwood (2017)
- *What I Know for Sure*, Oprah Winfrey (2014)
- *Wouldn't Take Nothing for My Journey Now*, Maya Angelou (1993)
- *Year of Yes: How to Dance It Out, Stand in the Sun and Be Your Own Person*, Shonda Rhimes (2015)

Podcasts

- Freakonomics Radio
- How I Built This
- How To Do Everything
- Power Hour
- Revisionist History
- TED Talks Daily
- The Debrief
- The Naked Scientists
- The Tim Ferriss Show
- Unlocking Us
- Where Should We Begin?
- You Are Not So Smart

Online Resources

- Bitch Media
- Business Insider
- Bustle
- Dazed Digital
- Fast Company's 30-Second MBA
- Forbes Magazine
- gal-dem
- Harvard Business Review
- Inc. Magazine
- Longform
- Longreads
- McKinsey
- New York Times
- TED-Ed
- The Cut

ENDNOTES

Introduction

p. 7 'As I write …', 'UK unemployment rate continues to surge', *BBC News*, 10 November 2020.

p. 7 'In a 2016 …', Bernard Salt, 'Evils of the hipster café', *The Australian*, 15 October 2016.

p. 8 'In fact, the …', 'The avocado toast index: How many breakfasts to buy a house?', *BBC Worklife*, 30 May 2017.

p. 8 'In her viral …', Anne Helen Petersen, 'How Millennials Became the Burnout Generation', *Buzzfeed News*, 5 January 2019.

p. 9 'Burnout', definition taken from World Health Organization, 'Burn-out an "occupational phenomenon": International Classification of Diseases', published 28 May 2019, available on who.int.

p. 9 'Erin Griffith wrote …', Erin Griffith, 'Why Are Young People Pretending to Love Work?', *New York Times*, 26 January 2019.

p. 10 'Petersen largely concludes that …', Petersen, op. cit.

p. 11 'In his 2019 …', Alex Collinson, 'The toxic fantasy of the "side hustle"', *Prospect Magazine*, 19 August 2019.

p. 12 'Opportunity cost', definition taken from *A Dictionary of Accounting*, ed. Jonathan Law (Oxford: Oxford University Press, 2016). Available on oxfordreference.com.

p. 12 'Every moment of …', Jenny Odell, *How to Do Nothing: Resisting the Attention Economy* (New York: Melville House, 2019).

Chapter One: Finding Your Purpose

p. 23   'the reason for which ...', 'a person's sense of ...', definitions taken from Google's English dictionary provided by Oxford Languages.

p. 25   'ran a LinkedIn survey ...', Lauren Vesty, 'Millennials want purpose over paychecks. So why can't we find it at work?', *Guardian*, 14 September 2016.

p. 25   'Dr Harris argues ...', Russ Harris, *The Happiness Trap: Stop Struggling, Start Living* (London: Constable & Robinson, 2007).

p. 28   'Multi-hyphenate', definition taken from Emma Gannon, *The Multi-Hyphen Method: Work Less, Create More: How to make your side hustle work for you* (London: Hodder & Stoughton, 2018).

p. 28   'We all have ...', Elaine Welteroth, quoted in Phoebe Lovatt, *The Working Woman's Handbook: Ideas, Insights, and Inspiration for a Successful Creative Career* (London: Prestel, 2017).

p. 29   'It's very likely ...', Cindy Blackstock, workshop at the National Indian Child Welfare Association Conference, 2014.

p. 29   'The realisation or ...', definition taken from Lexico.com by Oxford University Press, 2020.

p. 30   'There is no glory ...', Eve Ewing, quoted in Elaine Welteroth, *More Than Enough: Claiming Space for Who You Are (No Matter What They Say)* (London: Ebury Press, 2019).

p. 31   'Emma Gannon's list ...', from a tweet by Emma Gannon (@EmmaGannon), 13 February 2020.

p. 33   'in Welteroth's words ...', Welteroth, quoted in Lovatt, op. cit.

p. 33   'Flow', definition taken from Mihaly Csikszentmihalyi, *Flow: The Psychology of Optimal Experience* (New York: Harper and Row, 1990).

p. 34   '10,000-hours rule', definition taken from Daniel Levitin, quoted in Malcolm Gladwell, *Outliers: The Story of Success* (London: Allen Lane, 2008).

Chapter Two: The Productivity Method

p. 42   'Working smart', definition taken from Morten Hansen, 'Working Smart – Defined by a Study of Over 5,000 Managers and Employees', *Thrive Global*, 20 June 2018.

p. 43   'Tim Ferriss's 4-hour ...', Timothy Ferriss, *The 4-Hour Work Week: Escape the 9–5, Live Anywhere and Join the New Rich* (New York: Crown Publishers, 2007).

p. 44   'Deep work', definition from Cal Newport, *Deep Work: Rules for Focused Success in a Distracted World* (London: Piatkus, 2016).

p. 46   'Ferriss sums up ...', Ferriss, op. cit.

p. 55   'Deep work is ...', Newport, op. cit.

p. 56   'non-cognitively demanding ...', ibid.

p. 63   'Entrepreneur Steve Olenski ...', Steve Olenski, quoted in John Rampton, '15 Ways to Increase Productivity at Work', *Inc.com*, 4 February 2015.

p. 63   'According to a study ...', Rachel Emma Silverman, 'Workplace Distractions: Here's Why You Won't Finish This Article', *Wall Street Journal*, 11 December 2012.

p. 66   'Pareto's Principle', definition taken from Richard Koch, *The 80/20 Principle: The Secret of Achieving More with Less* (London: John Murray Press, 1997).

p. 70   'James Clear's book ...', James Clear, *Atomic Habits: An Easy & Proven Way to Build Good Habits & Break Bad Ones* (London: Random House Business, 2018).

p. 71   'in his theory ...', ibid.

Chapter Three: Let It Flow

p. 78   'Boreout', definition taken from Pablo Vandenabeele, quoted in Lauren Geall, 'Boreout: how to spot the tell-tale signs and what you can do about it', *Stylist*, 11 August 2020.

p. 80   'The concept of flow ...', Mihaly Csikszentmihalyi, *Flow: The Psychology of Optimal Experience* (New York: Harper and Row, 1990).

p. 80   Diagram on this page adapted from Csikszentmihalyi, op. cit.

p. 83   'According to Csikszentmihalyi ...', ibid.

p. 84   'Csikszentmihalyi also suggests ...', ibid.

p. 84   'If challenges are ...', ibid.

p. 102 'Echo chamber', definition taken from Lexico.com by Oxford University Press, 2020.

Chapter Four: Defining Success

p. 114 'who we are ...', Malcolm Gladwell, *Outliers: The Story of Success* (Allen Lane, 2008).

p. 128 Diagram on this page adapted from an Instagram post by Dr Nicole LePera (@the.holistic.psychologist), 2 May 2020.

p. 129 'Impostor syndrome', definition taken from Audrey Ervin, quoted in Abigail Abrams, 'Yes, Impostor Syndrome Is Real. Here's How to Deal With It', *Time*, 20 June 2018.

p. 130 'inner thermostat setting', Gay Hendricks, *The Big Leap: Conquer Your Hidden Fear and Take Life to the Next Level* (New York: HarperOne, 2009).

Chapter Five: Redefining Productivity

p. 142 '*karoshi* is the …', Justin McCurry, 'Japanese woman "dies from overwork" after logging 159 hours of overtime in a month', *Guardian*, 5 October 2017.

p. 142 'In 2019 (while …', Trade Unions Congress, 'British workers putting in longest hours in the EU, TUC analysis finds', issued 17 April 2019, available on tuc.org.uk.

p. 142 'compared to any …', Alan Jones, 'British workers put in longest hours in EU, study finds', *Independent*, 17 April 2019.

p. 142 'Taking a look …', Alanna Petroff and Océane Cornevin, 'France gives workers "right to disconnect" from office email', *CNN Business*, 2 January 2017.

p. 143 'divvy up jobs …', Jacinda Ardern, quoted in Karen Foster, 'The day is dawning on a four-day work week', *The Conversation*, 4 June 2020.

p. 146 'In her essay …', Jia Tolentino, 'The I in Internet', *Trick Mirror: Reflections on Self-Delusion* (London: Fourth Estate, 2019).

Chapter Six: Having It All

p. 153 'In her 1982 …', Helen Gurley Brown, *Having It All: Love, Success, Sex, Money, Even if You're Starting With Nothing …* (New York: Simon & Schuster, 1982).

p. 157 'when single women …', Sali Hughes, 'Helen Gurley Brown: how to have it all', *Guardian*, 14 August 2012.

p. 157 'Yet in a survey …', Equality and Human Rights Commission, 'Employers in the dark ages over recruitment of pregnant women and new mothers', published 19 February 2018, available on equalityhumanrights.com.

p. 166 'Self-sabotage', definition taken from Dr Judy Ho, *Stop Self-Sabotage: Six Steps to Unlock Your True Motivation, Harness Your Willpower, and Get Out of Your Own Way* (New York: HarperCollins, 2019).

Chapter Seven: The Art of Doing Nothing

p. 171 'that Thomas Edison …', Olga Khazan, 'Thomas Edison and the Cult of Sleep Deprivation', *The Atlantic*, 14 May 2014.

p. 181 'I loved Caroline …', Caroline O'Donoghue, 'Stop Pretending Your Flakiness Is Self-Care', *Grazia*, 1 May 2018.

p. 187 'reward-seeking, lab …', Jia Tolentino, 'The I in Internet', *Trick Mirror: Reflections on Self-Delusion* (London: Fourth Estate, 2019).

p. 189 'In Jenny Odell's …', Jenny Odell, *How to Do Nothing: Resisting the Attention Economy* (New York: Melville House, 2019).